Organizing Your Youth Soccer Team

Second Edition

Return to:

Jackson Christian
Elementary Intramurals

Organizing Your Youth Soccer Team
Second Edition

Swedish Soccer Federation

Compiled by—
Lars-Åke Backström, Tord Grip,
Roger Fridlund, Kenneth Karlsson,
Bjorn Westerberg

Translated from the Swedish
by Karl R. Nystrom

Leisure Press
Champaign, Illinois

Developmental Editor: Sue Ingels Mauck
Copy Editor: Claire Mount
Assistant Editor: JoAnne Cline
Production Director: Ernie Noa
Projects Manager: Lezli Harris
Typesetter: Brad Colson
Text Design: Keith Blomberg
Text Layout: Denise Mueller
Cover Design: Conundrum Designs
Cover Photo: Mary Messenger
Illustrations By: Dick Flood
Printed By: Versa Press

ISBN: 0-88011-300-6

Copyright © 1988, 1983 by Karl R. Nystrom

Library of Congress Cataloging-in-Publication Data

Fotbollsskolan. English.
  Organizing your youth soccer team.

  Translation of: Fotbollsskolan.
  Rev. ed. of: How to coach youth soccer.
  1. Soccer for children—Coaching. 2. Soccer for
children—Training. I. Backström, Lars-Åke.
II. Svenska fotbollsbundet. III. How to coach youth
soccer. IV. Nystrom, Karl R. V. Title.
GV943.8.F6913 1988   796.334'0240544   87-22535
ISBN 0-88011-300-6

Printed in the United States of America   10 9 8 7 6 5 4 3

Leisure Press
A Division of Human Kinetics
P.O. Box 5076, Champaign, IL 61825-5076
1-800-747-4457

Canada: Human Kinetics, Box 24040, Windsor, ON N8Y 4Y9
1-800-465-7301 (in Canada only)

Europe: Human Kinetics, P.O. Box IW14, Leeds LS16 6TR, England
0532-781708

Australia: Human Kinetics, P.O. Box 80, Kingswood 5062, South Australia
618-374-0433

New Zealand: Human Kinetics, P.O. Box 105-231, Auckland 1
(09) 309-2259

Acknowledgments

During the translation period, I had many opportunities to discuss this book, its approach, and the game and its future with many professional soccer players, coaches, and most important of all, the young players. These people gave me assurance that this type of a book would be useful especially to coaches starting out in the sport. I would like to thank all those people who assisted me: Patricia Poli, my editor, and John Griffin on the word processor. Most of all, many, many thanks go to my wife Ginger, who did endless hours of typing for this book. The translation became a labor of love, as well as a refresher course of the sport I grew up with.

Contents

Introduction

This book represents a fresh approach to coaching young soccer players. It gets away from the rigorous and technical approach advocated in many other soccer books and is directed toward actual play practice using small teams. Young players must practice more than specific techniques and endurance in order to fully gain good knowledge and understanding of the game. They should have the opportunity to play in game situations in all practice sessions.

There are many reasons to start a soccer program in a community that does not have one. We know that youth soccer is growing throughout the United States where there has been very little soccer activity at the adult level. We are presently realizing a phenomenal growth in the sport. In the United States, the challenge for the next five to ten years will be to keep the interest level high among our youth and not to lose too many players to more traditional sports. When a program is correctly run and well organized, the activity becomes fun for the children and gives them an everlasting interest in the sport. In addition, a well-run program improves the level of the sport. It is essential to plan year-round activities for everyone who desires such a program. Most importantly, it is more fun to play from the team's as well as the the individual child's points of view, when everyone has a good understanding of the game and can master the basic skills. Finally, the activity fills a social function. The children have something that is fun to do while learning good sportsmanship and teamwork.

The Swedish version of this book was compiled by a group of experienced Swedish soccer players, coaches, and educators, and was designed to be used by a typical Swedish soccer club. As translator, I have tried my best to adapt this work to soccer club activities and team coaching.

This book is divided into three parts. Covered in part I, Administrative Concerns, are the more general topics related to coaching soccer: coaching philosophy, goal setting, communication, organizing a new or existing program, and similar topics. In part II, Instructional Guide, the mechanics of setting up and directing practice sessions are discussed. Included in this part are elements of good offensive and defensive play, use of practice space, key concepts to emphasize during practices, and how to account for player size and skill level. In part III, Exercises, specific exercises for nine skill areas are presented. For each skill area one set of exercises is provided for seven- to nine-year-olds, and another for ten- to fourteen-year-olds. The exercises appear in an order based on level of difficulty, starting with the most basic. Included in each exercise are equipment requirements and practice field dimensions. Use the first two parts of this book to help you set up and organize your soccer program and practices. Then choose from part III those exercises that will be of most value to your players.

Part I

Administrative Concerns

1

To Be a Coach

As an active coach, you will have the task of caring for young people and helping them grow as individuals. It is your task to guide the players toward their potential. This includes physical ability, attitude, goals, and psychological attributes. To master this job you must, as a coach, understand your own personal view of the task. You must develop a philosophy of your coaching concept.

The word *philosophy* comes from the Greek language and means "love of wisdom" (*filein* = love, *sofia* = wisdom). To develop a philosophy means that one consciously tries to get a true picture of reality through study and experience. It is always important to first develop one's own philosophy, taking into account new experiences and new findings.

People Outlook

It is important that you have a positive outlook about people. Your behavior towards the players should be built on *understanding, mutual trust, and a general good feeling about each other*. A harmonic relationship between you and the players cannot be realized if you look at them as objects. You must treat the players as separate and unique individuals. Take the time to talk with, and take interest in, them as individuals.

This chapter was compiled by Mats Karlsson, Stefan Regfeldt, and Anders Torstensson under the direction of Bert Aggestedt at the Physical Education Department, College of Halmstad, Sweden.

Through other people's observations of you and your behavior, you can form a picture of yourself. This self-understanding is created through your cooperation with others. Identity, in other words, is not a trait, but rather a relationship. Instead of looking for a player's abilities, it is important that you, the coach, study the player's relationship to others.

Avoid looking at the players as working machines or empty barrels that should be filled with something. Every player is a reflecting and thinking person who has his or her own unique potential for success.

Unfortunately, as coaches, we often have predetermined opinions about our players' abilities. There is a myth about the importance of inheritance (e.g., one inherits ball sense); we believe that this is false. It is true, however, that different players have different talent levels and abilities. This relates, perhaps to many factors such as relationships and contacts the individual has had with sports in previous years. Generic inheritance plays a smaller role.

One should replace the weakness of a player with a positive people outlook. Strong self-assurance stimulates and encourages whereas a negative outlook crimps and holds back. It is not the result in itself that affects self-assurance; it is how one interprets one's contributions. Therefore, it is not knowledge of one's weakness that creates poor self-esteem, but rather the feeling of being weak. As a coach, it is important to give the players the opportunity to weld (stabilize and improve) themselves.

To weld oneself involves the following:

- Develop a sports philosophy.
- Motivate positively.
- Set goals.
- Learn within the sport.
- Communicate.

Sports Philosophy

To lead and develop youth through the most critical years of physical, mental, and human development is one of your most important tasks as a coach. You, perhaps more than any other instructor, are in an excellent position to succeed in that task.

Your sports philosophy must gel with your philosophy of life. To win games has been for a long time the yardstick of coaching success. Certainly the will to win has an important purpose in the development of sporting youths. As a coach, you must also emphasize the development of the youth as a real person. Your players come first, winning is second.

Dietmar Cramer, the famous West German soccer coach, provides his opinion of athletes and victory in the following quote:

Many of us overemphasize winning! Youth coaches must understand that boys and girls firstly want to have fun, but we (the coaches) have a totally different point of view on life and important things. For us, winning and success are most important. For small boys and girls the feeling of happiness is more important than the victory. To play is more important than to win. Youth can be more or less talented in playing the game. What you must give them as a starter is technique and, as you go along, talent. Everything else will come later. We must remember to build slowly and not to judge the youth with our adult measuring stick.

Positive Motivation

You will get more out of players by supporting them than you will by punishing them. That does not mean that you should praise every situation. The nature of sports is such that a certain amount of firmness is necessary, and the coach must set the limits.

We assume that most coaches use a combination of positive and negative reinforcements. Some coaches believe that they use a good combination, but they do not openly express their positive feelings. They do not praise the players because they believe that if the players do well, they do not need praise—they know when they do well.

Some believe that it is unnecessary to praise the obvious, but the players have no idea what the coach is thinking. They are only aware of their coach's critique. Few players have been spoiled by compliments, but many talented youths have quit sports due to the coach's constant criticism. To motivate your players, you must first help them recognize what, why, and how they should practice. Ultimately, you want them to be self-motivated and thus to realize why practice is necessary.

Motivation is not an instinct. People create their own motivation levels in cooperation with others. As a coach, you have the important task of seeing that this cooperation is working. You and the players must support and encourage each other.

To succeed, your coaching must be built on the players' positive images of themselves. They must know that they can do it. If you constantly give negative criticism, you can't expect your players to maintain positive images of themselves and their abilities. The following are some suggestions for building positive self-images:

- Start out with praise. Mention a situation in which they did well (be honest). This will help the players, and soon they will be able to take criticism in situations where they do not do so well.
- Execute the correction or instruction. You must be accurate concerning the criticism and honest towards the players regardless of what they do and how it should be done more effectively.
- Finish with a compliment. Finally, you should stress to the players that with practice they will improve their weaknesses because they are good and coachable players.

Goal Setting

Long-range planning is necessary to achieve success, but it must be flexible. Goals are set for live human beings, and we know people change as they develop.

Because coaching is related to individuals as a whole, you as a coach must understand the players' physical composition, how they function, their mental and inner attitude, and how they interrelate with others.

You can obtain information from many sources (e.g., critical observations at games and practices and talks with parents). You must know what you should observe and why. Make a list and follow the player's progress frequently. The following example will give you an idea of what to record:

After six weeks of training, John should be willing to shoot with his left foot as well as with his right, but not necessarily with the same ability and accuracy. By mid-season Jay will cut his time on fifty yards by one-half second.

You should find out three things about your players at the start of a season.

- What experience do they have?
- What can they handle today?
- What would they like to accomplish?

When you know the answers, you and your team can work toward a united goal.

Goals and partial goals form the basis of your plan. They will clarify what you are planning for and will determine what you choose from all the information and experience you have gathered. The ideal situation occurs whenever you and the players can establish goals and partial goals, and work together toward these goals. Because the players will get older and obtain more experience, you should let them participate in this goal-setting exercise.

Goals are set for the long range. They should be difficult but not impossible to reach. Partial goals are short range and form the building blocks of the long-range goals. As they reach short-range goals, players can see progress, both as individuals and as a team. This process also reinforces the importance and the accessibility of the long-range plan.

To Learn Within the Sport

One of your concerns as a coach should be that the teaching process progresses as well as possible. One of the many important factors of effective teaching is the atmosphere in which the coaching takes place. The surroundings, or coaching aura, will be affected by methods, materials, and personnel. The humanistic atmosphere created by you, the coach, can enhance or destroy the team's capability to learn.

The result depends both on what should be taught and who is teaching. The speed of learning varies for different persons and situations; some players need more time to learn than others. At the start, it is also important to remember that success will come easier as your coaching develops; then there will be times when you feel that progress is slow, perhaps nonexistent. This creates an uneasiness for some coaches, who may even change their programs because they think that something isn't working.

The feeling of reaching a plateau is normal. It is important to remember that, if the team's playing style is correct and fair, then teaching methods have been effective up to this point; there is no reason to panic. Stagnation will pass, and the effect of instruction will show in increased team strength.

The exercises at practice should be challenging. Exercises that are challenging to some players will not be challenging to others. Therefore you should change the exercises so that they do not become boring. A good coaching situation is realized whenever the players see the meaning in what you ask them to do. In other words, they should see the connection between the exercise and its application to actual soccer playing.

The coaching atmosphere should encourage experimentation and new ideas. Many coaches become easily stereotyped in their thinking and use the same coaching methods year after year. It is important to be flexible in your coaching system and open to new ideas. The best learning situation depends, therefore, on the atmosphere that you and your players can create and on the methods and materials available to you.

Communication

Communication is the transfer of information, attitudes, and feelings from one person to another. It can take place through the spoken language as well as through facial expressions, body positions, gestures, and voice tone.

You should avoid unnecessary gestures, mimics, and the like. These can be misinterpreted by the players. It is easy to put down a player unconsciously through miscommunication. Clear communication should be the goal in your work. The art of understanding and listening are also important skills to develop.

You must be aware that some of your players will need special handling or special forms of communication. Tending to this special communication is as important as technique and skill training. In all situations your effective communication skill with the players is the key to success.

Successful communication is based on a combination of knowledge and respect for the players with whom you communicate. The foundation of all forms of communication is respect and trust. The most effective communication happens in a one-to-one dialogue between you and a player. Poor communication takes place when other disturbing elements are present and distract a player (spectators, other activities on the field, players, etc.).

After they make a mistake, the players will be the least open to communication. Most people are very timid after they make a mistake. If you try to communicate at this time you will encounter resistance and hostility. Be sensitive to this fact as you attempt to correct your players' mistakes.

In general, try to make eye contact when you communicate with the players. Always listen to them; each player should feel that he or she has the freedom to express his or her point of view without being punished.

2

How to Organize a Coaching Program

Coaching activities may be set up many ways, but you should organize the activities so that they suit your team's ideas and goals. Do your own thing in such a way that you take into consideration parents' and community resources, playing fields, transportation, and so on.

Talk to the club and to as many other experienced coaches as possible. Use their advice at your own discretion.

Plan systematically. A plan such as the one in Figure 2.1, often used in business-related activities, is very useful in sports activities.

1. Analyze the present conditions of your club.

Within your group, address your present conditions at a question-and-answer session, and make sure to discuss activities that are of interest to the whole group. Include resources, problems, and possibilities of the group.

- What fields and facilities may be used?
- Do you have enough balls and other necessary equipment?
- What is your financial position?
- What is the players' level of interest?
- Within a club, what are the different girl/boy age groupings?
- How high an interest level do the club board members have?

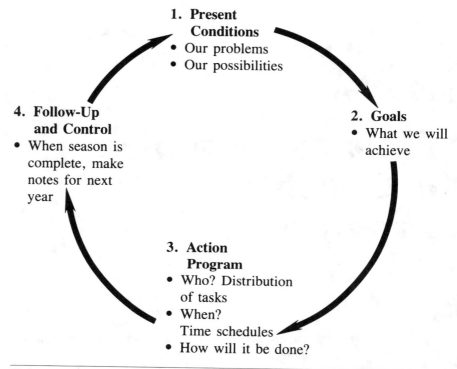

Figure 2.1 Planning strategy.

- What is the interest level of other people in the community?
- At what level is the interest in the sport within your community center, other sports-oriented organizations, and the high school administration?
- How about the possible involvement of other community groups such as Lions, Rotary, and Kiwanis clubs?
- Are there any other as yet untapped resources?

2. Establish realistic goals for this activity.

All activities to which you, the coach, donate your time should have realistic, measurable goals with set time limits. The following are examples of the short- and long-range goals of a new club during its first season.

Short-range goals for the beginning of the season:

- Within two months the club will have two coaching clinics with at least twenty participants in each clinic.
- New coaches will attend at least one of the clinics.

Long-range goal for the end of the season:

- 50 percent of all coaches will have participated in a clinic.

All goals must be realistic, measurable, and regularly reevaluated.

A successful sport activity can seldom be managed from the top (i.e., a large organization). Its design must come from the bottom. People within the community will be more in touch with the needs of the activity and should be encouraged to participate.

3. Devise an action program.

If you have analyzed the present conditions accurately, you will be able to discuss step by step what can be done as well as what must be done both now and in the future.

Once you have a plan, you must put together some detailed action programs that identify the task, who will perform it, and when it must be accomplished. The following are examples of action programs.

Who?	For a New Club	Last Date
KEN	Get all field assignments	6/12
ERIC	Print invitations for mailing	7/1
CARL	Do the mailing	7/5
Who?	For a Team	Last Date
JIM	Get out field assignments	7/16
JOHN	Get cones and other materials	7/21
SARAH	Set up phone callers	7/25

4. Plan follow-up and control measures.

With clear goals and detailed programs, you may now check the situation at preset interims. After the season is over, you should go back to your original programs to check the following:

- Have you reached your goals?
- How have you reached your goals?
- What changes should be made in the future?

This follow-up will then become the basis for next year's goals and program.

Facilities, Leaders, and Funds

The greatest problem for any team sport activity is acquiring facilities, coaches, referees, and funds. The following are a few suggestions for attacking this problem.

Facilities

School facilities are usually not used after 4:00 p.m. Discuss your program with the school administrators. If it is a new activity in your community, let them know what you are up to. There are usually solutions to all problems.

Leaders

In many clubs there are shortages of coaches, referees, and managers.

- Use the talent that is available in the community as efficiently as possible. Every task will be less time-consuming for each individual.
- Give everyone a clear job description. It should be easier to attract potential leaders if they know exactly what is expected of them.
- Go to the outside (e.g., friends and parents) if necessary. Remember, there are many tasks that do not require knowledge of the game.
- The activities will be better if, instead of one or two people doing everything, you involve more people doing smaller tasks.

Funds

Should the managers, referees, and coaches be reimbursed? Small payments could increase the interest level of the job. If you decide to pay these participants, you need to resolve all expenses at the start of the season. Everyone concerned should participate in establishing the budget. It is often necessary to go out and look for contributions. Local merchants are still the best source. Discuss with parents how much it is worth to them to have their children participating in a well-organized sport activity. Establish fees in cooperation with the parents.

Parent Participation

Often, the only contact parents have with the club is paying for dues and uniforms. A good soccer club is not just a place where parents can send kids for some activity. (Your coach is not running a baby-sitting service.) Whenever you start a soccer activity, you should emphasize the theme of *Soccer Together*—parents and children. The purpose is to inform, activate, and recruit help and let parents participate in the children's leisure activities.

We believe that motivation to come along and pull together as manager, coach, and participant increases the knowledge of what the sport can give one's child. If goal setting to involve parents is to succeed, there must be some work from the team leaders' side. It is you who can reach the parents. It is you who must convince them that shared joy is double joy.

Evening Meetings

The first step in initiating a program is to meet and talk with the parents. Many clubs/teams start out with an evening meeting. Let's look at some experiences you can build on.

Plan Ahead

Plan meetings at a time that causes the fewest conflicts (e.g. not on practice nights, Super Bowl night, or on the night of some big local sport event). It is impossible to avoid all conflicts, but with planning you should get the new club/team parents involved from the beginning. For a large meeting, especially if the players are involved, arrange for a soccer movie (there are many available through different sources). Invite the parents personally (do not send messages through the players).

Content of the Meeting

The goal of a meeting is to give the parents information about the club/team and to increase their interest. Keep the presentation positive; don't focus on the problems involved or you might discourage the parent participation that you seek.

The following is an example of an evening meeting agenda:

1. Greet parents and introduce coordinators.
2. Discuss objectives of youth sports (ten minutes).
3. Give the details of your soccer program (ten minutes).
4. Explain coaching roles and relationships (ten minutes).
5. Outline parents' roles and responsibilities (twenty minutes).
6. Close with a question-and-answer period (thirty minutes).
7. Take a break (provide refreshments).
8. Show a movie.

Economy

A large evening meeting requires some planning, but try to keep your costs down. The following expenses should be included in your planning:

- Written invitations and telephone calls
- Rental of facility
- Refreshments (coffee, cake, cookies, etc.)
- Movie rental (some are available at no charge)

The purpose of this type of meeting is to get the parents together and give them some insight into upcoming activities. Always budget some funds for these meetings.

Follow-Up

Finally, encourage the parents to meet again, for example, after a practice sometime in the next few weeks. This follow-up will allow them to grow into the club slowly, without feeling that they are being forced into activities.

Part II

Instructional Guide

3 ⚽

To Play Soccer

Great soccer players like Pelé, Beckenbauer, and Kyle Rote, Jr. became great by playing constantly ever since they were small children. They were always playing with the ball and creating small game situations (i.e., one-on-one or two-on-two). Pelé would never have been the player he was, had he stood for hours practicing trapping the ball and making ground passes without actually creating real play situations with his friends.

What Is Most Important?

Look at what kids do whenever they get out on a field with a ball. Find out how you can get to know what they experience at that time. If the player is alone, he or she will try to take shots against some kind of backdrop (baseball cage, etc.). With a friend, one becomes goalie. If they find more friends, one or two usually take charge and now you have two small teams, playing against one or two goals.

Their most important experiences are

- to challenge someone else for the ball, and
- to score goals.

Therefore, you should give the players the opportunity to do both of these. Unfortunately, there is a big difference between small game situations and team/club playing. This difference makes it difficult to provide your players

Figure 3.1 Informal play is an important part of learning.

Figure 3.2 Small game situations.

with the two experiences above. A comparison between the two situations makes this clear.

The Children's Soccer World	The Team/Club World
Small spaces	Large fields
Small groups	Nine to eighteen kids at one time
Many chances to score goals	Few goal scoring chances
All are participating	The best players are very active, and consequently lower level players hardly participate at all
No prescribed player positions	Often fixed positions

How Should You Coach?

What ideas should youth coaches work with to encourage young players' hopes while being an effective coach? There are two basic rules:

- The practice should simulate a game as closely as possible.
- Coaching of techniques isolated from game situations should be avoided.

Therefore, playing with direction should be the basic aim. The players then meet the requirements of the game; namely they judge their own, as well as the opposing teams' positions and movements; place themselves, move, and receive passes under pressure from other players; and take the ball away from and pressure opponents. In addition, whenever they get the ball from opponents, players start or continue an attack under pressure from other players. Finally, at all times players are in a decision-making and problem-solving situation.

What Is Play Practice?

Play practice entails playing with small teams on small playing areas with smaller and lighter balls.

You should base your coaching on this small team approach, which places

Figure 3.3   Play with direction.

your players in game-like situations. This approach has the following advantages:

- There are teammates and opposing players.
- The practice has direction against one or two goals.
- The players get experience from different exposures.
- The players on small teams have more opportunities to participate than on big teams.
- The players can often finish a play.

Through small team coaching, you teach these four general skills:

- Comprehension of the game: the ability to guess the next move, take the correct position, and play away from the ball (on the field).
- Passing techniques: the ability to pass in play situations by knowing how, when, and where to pass, and by recognizing the movements of teammates and opposing team players. The players will be able to decide whether to use the inside or outside of the foot depending on which they consider best for a given situation.
- Conditioning: the ability to work hard in small game practice and consequently build up enough conditioning to play a full game.
- Speed: the ability to play at game speed situations suitable for soccer.

Additions to Play Practice

Additions to play coaching must also be considered. It is useful to single out the players from the practice session and give them some extra attention concerning skill acquisition.

Figure 3.4 Passing techniques.

Heading

In play practice there is a tendency to keep the ball on the ground because it is easier to handle the ball this way. In a match, there are corner kicks, free kicks, goal kicks, and so on. Therefore, all heading practice should simulate game situations.

Figure 3.5 Heading.

Shots on Goal and Other Finishes

Because the difference between success and failure in soccer depends on scoring goals and/or finishing an attack, proper shooting practice should be stressed.

Figure 3.6 Goalie plays.

Goalie Plays

You must give the team's most important player opportunities to practice and develop talents that are needed during a game. Give the goalkeeper training that comes as close to game situations as possible by using both attackers and defenders during practices.

How About Technique?

A common question coaches ask is "should we first teach players to make a proper instep pass or an outside-of-the-foot pass before we start play practice?" This traditional coaching method often places two players facing each other, passing back and forth. The result of this drilling of technique is that the players become very proficient in practice but cannot adapt to real game situations.

Traditionally, the comparison has been made between soccer talent and soccer technique. A talented player was required to master the basics: passing, stopping, dribbling, and heading. If soccer talent is interpreted only in this way, there is a tendency to practice these tasks in such a way that they are isolated from the game itself.

Soccer technique should never be an isolated task. To control the ball completely is of little value for a player who cannot comprehend the correct moment to use the acquired technique. The dominating factor in assessing a good player is his or her ability to execute properly in the given situation and to interpret the requirements of the total situation and decide upon the correct solution.

It does not help to isolate the instep pass if you do not practice it in conjunction with why, where, and when the pass should be made. Passing skills should always be practiced in game situations. It is up to the player to decide when and in what direction the pass should be made. This decision is dependent on the field position of teammates and opposing players. Passing with the inside or outside of the foot then becomes academic, and the player must come up with the best solution.

In play practice, as opposed to isolated technique practice, the player has the opportunity to practice all different types of passes; this simulates true game situations. Additionally, play practice gives players the opportunity for self-instruction and experience.

The improvements in the players come from the opportunity to see and gather experiences required in changing play situations. Even though your instructions are important, true learning is achieved through the experience gained by playing the game.

Figure 3.7   Practice passing skills in game situations.

4

Basics of Offensive and Defensive Play

T he emphasis in play practice should be on offense. As soon as the team has learned the basics of offense, you should move into defensive play. Set up the practices so that the attacking team always has a numerical advantage. This will make it easier to teach different offensive situations, and many goals will be scored. To create many situations and to finish an attack, the players must have good passing plays going between them.

Offensive Play

The number one requirement for a good passing game is to have the players in correct *play distance*. Distance should not be too close or too far for the defense to break up the attack (Figures 4.1 and 4.2).

For a good passing game, the pass receivers should place themselves in a position to receive a pass. They should be able to move without the ball and avoid the *passing shadow* behind an opposing player (Figure 4.3).

The ball handler should give the opposing player a difficult time. Instead of passing the ball to a teammate, he or she might fake a pass and drive

Figure 4.1 Poor play distance.

Figure 4.2 Good play distance.

Figure 4.3 Avoid the passing shadow.

Figure 4.4 Offensive maneuver: pass feint.

with the ball in another direction. Such a *pass feint* (Figure 4.4) gives the player an alternative to outplay the opposition.

The players should also understand the term *play depth*: The ball handler should have teammates in front of as well as behind him or her (Figure 4.5).

To keep the ball within the team, the players must be able to make the *back pass* (Figure 4.6). Whenever a forward or side pass is too risky and there is a possibility of losing possession of the ball, the back pass is most effective.

In addition, thinking about *play width* is required (Figure 4.7). This is used to pull the defenders apart so you can go through or around the other players.

Figure 4.5 Play depth.

Figure 4.6 Back pass.

Figure 4.7 Play width.

Defensive Play

Good defensive play builds on discipline and organization as well as the following:

- Changing quickly from attack to defense whenever the other team gets the ball.
- Moving to the defensive side of the respective opposing player.
- Pressuring the ball handler by the closest player to stop him or her from driving with the ball or executing a good pass.

Figure 4.8 Pressuring the ball handler.

Figure 4.9 Support.

- Understanding the meaning and importance of support. If the pressuring player is outplayed, there should be immediate support from a teammate to pressure the attacking ball handler.

- Marking (assuming the proper defensive position) so that the defending player can break up a pass before the attacker can gain control of the ball.
- Covering areas on the field that are open to the attacking team.

Figure 4.10 Marking.

Figure 4.11 Covering.

5 ⚽

Instruction in Play Practice

As an instructor, it is your job to teach players a good understanding of the game and its basic principles. Instruction by play practice is an excellent method for achieving this as long as you give clear directions. Play practice lets the players learn for themselves. In turn, you are freed up to walk around and observe the different groups in small games. This gives you the added opportunity of giving direction where it is most needed.

It is very difficult to instruct properly on a big field with eleven-player games in progress. Instruction is easier, and the players can be seen in an overview, when you use fewer players such as two against two or five against five. In these situations it is easier to see your instruction points materialize.

If some points of attack play are practiced, give the attackers a numerical advantage. It creates a situation in which it is easier for the attackers to penetrate and finish the play situation. That will consequently ease your coaching.

It is also possible to create methodical increases in coaching. Instead of three against three, you can give the attackers the advantage of playing three against one with goalies on each side. The defending team has only one player and a goalie. You will then finish the practice with a goal, a goalie save, a shot that misses, or a defender's playing back to his or her own goalie.

After practicing the attack play, change the pattern so that the defender becomes the attacker. Two other players change teams for this new attack. When you need more of a challenge for the attacker, simply increase the defense to two players and a goalie.

As you progress, you can change the situation by organizing larger teams, but always let the attacking team have a numerical advantage: four against three, five against three, or five against four to start with. After that you should continue the intensity and even up the teams. In a game, the attackers are many times up against a numerically stronger defense (so you can turn the tables and practice three against four as a final effort in this practice).

To achieve better results, you also should direct the play. If the intentions are to get the players to make a passing fake, play two against one and give an extra point to the team when a player executes a successful fake. Direct a small team play so that it is as valuable for the team to execute a successful passing fake as to score a goal. This motivates the players to actively look for situations in which a passing fake can be executed. Encourage the players to make the passing fake on a spot of the field that can result in a goal chance. This enables you to direct the play by giving higher points for goals that are the direct result of successful passing fakes.

The long-range goal of the exercises in the following chapters is to teach the players to execute a particular skill in seven-player and eleven-player games.

On the following pages we will give examples for conducting play practice by

- starting out with few players on the team;
- playing with the attacking team's having a numerical advantage (when attacking is practiced);
- directing the play;
- slowly increasing the number of players on each team; and
- changing the numerical relationship between the teams.

Example: Instruction of Wall Plays

When proceeding with your coaching program, you must decide, on the basis of the age and knowledge of your players, how quickly to introduce a new play.

For example, you may notice that your players are advancing in their skill levels and executing moves similar to a wall play. At this point, you should identify the instruction points that use the wall play and incorporate them into your program. Some of these points are listed here: A detailed explanation of a wall play exercise follows (see also chapter 9).

- The ball handler shall challenge (approach almost straight on) the opposing player before a pass is made to the wall.
- The passes must be accurate both ways.
- The wall should play directly (without stopping and controlling).
- The ball handler should, after passing to the wall, increase speed and rush past the opposing player.

Figure 5.1 Challenging the opposition.

Figure 5.2 Wall pass.

Organize teams of two against one plus a goalie on as many small areas as you can. The attacking team has two players and a numerical advantage. One player on the defending team is always goalie. Whenever the defenders get the ball, they should become the attackers and play two against one.

Figure 5.3 Two against one plus goalie.

Certainly you could choose to start the exercise by explaining the techniques of the wall play, but it is considered more effective to have the teams play until you see something that looks like a wall play, and then stop and freeze the play. Point out the wall play or what looks like a wall play. All players should remain still in their positions. Gather the rest of the team for demonstration.

• Try to use two-way communication. Activate discussion with the players through questions/answers to point out different highlights in the wall play. Stress the four given instruction points.
• Do not forget to give encouragement for every point the players earn.
• Do not give too many instructions at once.

The play then continues with instruction on how to use the wall play. Stop when you see the obvious. Gather the players, repeat past instructions, and add on new instructions.

To motivate the players to make wall passes, guide the play. Give one point (goal) for every successful wall play (i.e., when they overtake the other team). It then becomes as valuable to make a good wall play as to score a goal.

In the beginning, the two attackers should often succeed. After a while the defender will become more experienced and play smarter. He or she will get closer to the wall and thereby make it harder for the attacker to make the play. At that time you should move on.

• Stop the play and gather the players.
• Activate their thinking. Let them tell you in their own words why it is not so easy to make the wall play.

Figure 5.4 Dribble past the opponent.

- Ask them what countermoves the attackers can execute.
- Ask the players if there is any alternative to the wall play.

Even though you may know the answers to these questions, avoid presenting solutions (overinstructing). Give the players the opportunity to suggest their own ideas and solutions.

Perhaps the players themselves realize that the ball handler may choose not to pass to the wall, because that is just what the defense expects. You want the players to realize that the ball handler will drive the ball without passing. If he or she can complicate the situation for the defense through making a passing fake to the wall, he or she probably can finish the attack with a shot on goal.

Direct the play as follows:

- 3 points for a wall pass and a goal.
- 3 points for a fake wall pass, dribble by the defender, and then a goal.
- 1 point for a wall pass or faking a wall pass.
- 1 point for a goal by any other means.

If the wall pass still does not work properly, you can increase the numerical advantage for the attackers, add a player on each team, and play three against one plus two goalies.

Using this organization with teams of different sizes (i.e., numerically uneven), you can direct the play until the players are ready to practice wall plays in real games of seven- and eleven-person teams. Have patience. The step from wall plays in small teams to those in real game situations is cumbersome and requires perseverance and time.

Analysis

You must be able to analyze what happens in the play and see what your players can and can't do. If you start out a new season with players who have passed the beginner stage, it will help to play a game among yourselves with two small teams. It is then easier to analyze, if you use an analyzing guide. Let the result of the analysis be the basis for future coaching. Later on, you can use this guide in game practice as well as in real games.

Do the first analysis together with an experienced soccer coach who can easily detect the good as well as the bad habits of the players. Describe the playing patterns by putting numbers in areas where players should be. Even though this looks complicated, you will soon discover that the plays become more interesting when you learn to analyze them. Concentrate on one team at a time, otherwise it becomes very confusing.

You can also let your players make an analysis. Have a right wing analyze another right wing player, or have them study and analyze their friends.

An analysis schedule can be put together in different ways. See Tables 5.1 and 5.2 for suggestions.

The match (real game) is the goal of all practices. The purpose of the practice is to improve the players' and the team's performance in the match. The match should also be the basis of practice. Therefore, you should isolate the details and situations from the match that you feel should be practiced and improved.

Sometimes it is suitable to continue to improve on good execution by your team and/or players. Conversely, you can do it another way by

Table 5.1 Analysis Schedule for a Team

Attacking Plays	Defense
1. Are the plays functioning according to basic principles?	1. Are the plays functioning according to basic principles?
2. What attacking methods are used? Are there two-on-one situations? Are the players using wall plays, overlapping, and leaving?	• defensive side/goal side • press • support • marking • coverage
3. How are the individual performances coming through? Are they faking and dribbling?	

Table 5.2   Analysis Schedule for an Individual Player

1. What does the player do whenever he or she doesn't have the ball?
2. What does he or she do whenever he or she has the ball?
3. What does he or she do whenever the opponent has the ball?
4. What strong points does he or she have? What weak ones?
5. Is he or she moving quickly enough to help the ball handler avoid the passing shadow?
6. Does he or she miss passes often?
7. Can he or she fake the pass?
8. Can he or she pass back?
9. Can he or she press, give support, mark, and cover?

improving the weak executions. To do this, you must have the ability to analyze what is happening in a game. You must seek the reasons for success or failure at the games in all stages.

Reflection

Whenever you give instructions, you hope that the players will learn something. For coaching to be effective, the players must have the opportunity to reflect on what you tell them. This means that you give the players information during practice about how they are executing the movements. Players want to know if they are doing well.

Figure 5.5 The joys of scoring a goal.

In soccer practices, feedback takes place through verbal information. You tell the players how a coaching phase is done or shout the instructions during the play. Praise the players if they do well. If they don't, let them know. You must also give new instructions. If you repeat the same exercise and it goes well, then the players have learned something.

Effective feedback depends on the following:

- Be sensitive to whether or not your players are understanding your instructions. Although verbal instructions may be sufficient for some, others may need you to show them how to carry out a play.
- Give feedback using the proper soccer terminology (see Glossary). It is important to be specific about what the players are doing correctly and incorrectly.
- Provide immediate feedback. Any delay in your instruction after a play will decrease learning effectiveness.

Sometimes the players may have difficulties understanding the connection between your instructions and the play situations in which they are involved. When this happens, stop the play or freeze a situation to describe more clearly how, for instance, a given player moved out of the passing shadow and opened himself or herself up for a play. If you incorporate this coaching method, begin by isolating situations in which the players are doing something right. This emphasizes positive feedback, which has a higher reward level. How often should the play be stopped for continuous instructions? It is up to you, but, in general, the play-stops should be as few and short as possible.

Finally, you should avoid talking too much. Many players, especially those who are very young, are not yet mature enough to take a lot of verbal instruction. They cannot relate the spoken instruction to a specific situation in the game. With young players, you should give a short orientation of what the exercise should accomplish and then give ample time for them to try the exercise in play. It is naturally easier for a young player to see the practice executed than to understand your verbal description.

Talk in the Game

Encourage the players to develop the habit of talking during practice and in the game to help each other, as well as to guide and give instructions to each other.

The ability to talk constructively and to help teammates, especially the ball handler, is a very valuable asset. Most of the players, even the top players in the world, are too quiet on the field during a game.

Many young players have difficulty with talking. Rather than talk to their teammates, the players often develop selfish calls for passes. To overcome this, you have to teach them *what* to say and *when* to say it. If you teach players the habit of talking only in a few specific situations in addition to determining carefully what should be said, you will make it easier for them to communicate with one another.

Figure 5.6 Encourage talking on the field.

"Keep the Ball—Turn Up"

A player passing the ball should call "keep the ball" to the receiver if the opposing players are far away and cannot immediately attack the ball handler. The ideal is when the ball receiver, through a good overview before receiving the ball, becomes fully aware of the closest opposing player's position. You can develop this further by having the players call "turn up," if the receiver has the possiblity to turn into the attacking direction.

"Pass"

Whenever the receiver is pressed by an opposing player, he or she should say "pass". The pass receiver should be aware of his or her ball control abilities whenever he or she decides to keep or pass the ball.

Call For a Pass

Young players are often willing to ask for a pass from the ball handler. Sometimes this is done with poor judgment because they want to get hold of the ball.

The players should learn when to call for the ball. They should only call for a pass when they are moving to a position where they can be reached with a solid pass. Even here the ball handler should clarify the situation. The teammate's call gives him or her extra control. In an important situation, the ball handler may be able to see a good passing possibility; a call from the teammate can then create a better play situation.

If we can teach our players to realize how important it is to be able to talk in the game, we have taught them something very valuable.

6

Organization

In addition to organized soccer in clubs and schools, there should be opportunities for girls and boys to practice individually and with small teams.

The community, schools, and clubs can do this through leasing out all facilities available for soccer as often as possible, and creating many small areas where small team games can be held. Small team games are preferred over large team games (eleven vs. eleven, etc.). Practice with eleven-player teams occasionally, but limit these to older children (e.g., twelve-year-olds and up).

The *passing play* is the basis of all attacks and should be at the top of the list when you choose exercises. After that, you can practice feints and wall plays before you go into other attacks such as leaving and overlapping.

As mentioned earlier, the defensive plays should be started when the basics of the attacks are understood. Be flexible especially if you are the sole coach. However, defense should be practiced when the season approaches.

Playing with smaller balls for younger children should be mandatory as well as playing with a good indoor ball for indoor practice. Special indoor balls are now available on the market.

Soccer, one of the greatest participant sports, should be practiced year-round under most conditions. Outside practices in snow and cold are not the best for youth soccer, but indoor facilities are often available.

Planning and Organizing a Practice

This section will give you some examples of how you, as an instructor for a club or a team, can organize a practice session. You should know the following before you start the planning:

- the time allotted you
- the number of players
- the players' abilities
- the size of the field
- the number of balls available
- the number of helpers available
- the availability of other coaching aids

After this, you should ask yourself the following questions:

- *What should be practiced?* What do you want to achieve? The purpose of the practice will definitely affect the choice of exercises.
- *How should the drills be done?* The requirements are to reach a high level of activity, and thus the exercises should be repeated such that the effect of the practice becomes optimal.

To provide additional motivation for the players, you can establish time limits, or point scoring.

If you want to increase the level of difficulty, you can limit ball touches, or vary players' numerical advantages and disadvantages.

The next question to consider concerns the individual players:

- *Who should do what?* Who should practice in the same group? Who will take free kicks and corner kicks? Who will finish an attack? Who should attack and who should defend?

Finally—and this is true if you are thinking of different activities with many groups—you should know the following:

- *Where should the different activities be executed?* Where on the field, in reference to goals, lines, and surroundings, is the exercise best suited?

A coaching activity should always start with a warm-up activity. The square and number ball practices are samples of excellent warm-ups and openings. At all times, the players should practice passing, receiving, moving out of the passing shadow, and so on. After that, you should limit the session to a few exercises (one, two, or at the most, three).

Figure 6.1 Ball practices: square (top) and number (bottom).

How to Use the Exercises

The exercise suggestions are illustrated in this book for two age groups: seven to nine years and ten to fourteen years. The talent of your players should also determine your choice of exercises. If you have talented nine-year-old players with three years of experience, you could start using exercises for ten- to fourteen-year-olds. We recommend that the exercises be used in proper order, because we have tried to increase the difficulty as they progress.

Every exercise contains the headings Organization and Instructions. Under Organization, you will learn how the exercise is executed, and under Instructions, you will get help with instructions for the exercise.

Four cones should be used in almost all exercises and placed in the four corners of the playing area being used. They are drawn into the figures whenever they are needed to illustrate the area. In addition, the number of cones needed is listed. The recommended dimensions are in meters and can be adjusted to the field size available.

In all exercises, we have split the players in groups of 2, 3, 4, 6, 7, or 12. (This is based on a maximum group of 24). If you have groups of more than 24 players, you can solve it in different ways. For example: If you have 26 players, you can start the exercises letting one group play four against two. Remember, whenever you establish the groups, that it is more difficult to play four against two than it is to play three against one.

Sample Practice Sessions

Following are descriptions of several ways to set up practice sessions, including suggestions for using the available space. The examples include exercises presented in part III of this book.

Figure Legend

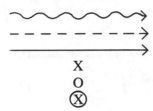

	the player's path with the ball
	the player's path without the ball
	the path of the ball
X	attacking player
O	defending player
Ⓧ	ball handler

Example 1

Age: Seven to nine years
Time: 40 minutes
Players: 26
Equipment: 8 balls, 24 cones
Area Sizes: 70 x 40 meters
Exercises: Seven to Nine years, Exercise 3, One Passing: 10 Minutes
            Seven to Nine years, Exercise 6, Two Passing: 30 Minutes

Passing for Seven- to Nine-Year-Olds, Exercise 3
Start with three against one in a square (See Figure 6.2 for a suggested practice layout).

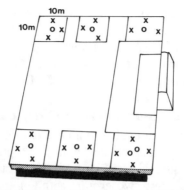

Figure 6.2 Three against one in a square (seven- to nine-year-olds).

Two, Passing, Seven to Nine Years, Exercise 6

Divide the players into four groups: six players in three groups and eight players in the fourth group. Play four against one plus two goalies for under thirty minutes on four areas according to the organization and instructions of Passing for seven- to nine-year-olds, Exercise 6, with the change that the fourth group play four against two plus two goalies. See Figure 6.3 for a suggested practice layout.

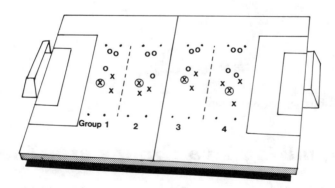

Figure 6.3 Passing (seven- to nine-year-olds).

Example 2

Age: Ten to Fourteen years
Time: 60 minutes
Players: 21

Equipment: 10 balls, 24 cones

Area sizes: 70 x 40 meters

Exercises: Ten to Fourteen Years, Exercise 1, One Passing: 10 Minutes
Ten to Fourteen Years, Exercise 8, Two Passing: 25 Minutes
Seven to Nine Years, Exercise 5, Three Passing: 25 Minutes

Passing for Ten- to Fourteen-Year-Olds, Exercise 1

Play in the square, five against two within a restricted area for under ten minutes. Change the exercise so that it suits the players by playing five against two in three squares. See Figure 6.4 for a suggested practice layout. Divide the players into two groups with ten and eleven players. Let each group have half of the area. Then one group practices Exercise 2 and the other Exercise 3. The groups change exercises after twenty-five minutes.

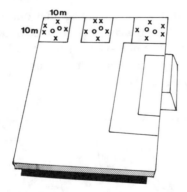

Figure 6.4 Five against two in three squares.

Organizing Two Groups at a Time

See Figures 6.5 and 6.6 for examples of field layouts when two groups are practicing at the same time. Further suggestions for utilizing field space are shown in Figures 6.7 and 6.8.

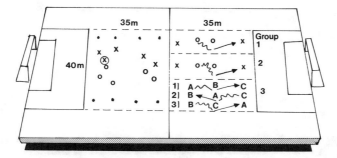

Figure 6.5 *Left half of field*: Players practice Passing for ten- to fourteen-year-olds, Exercise 8. *Right half of field*: Players practice Passing for seven- to nine-year-olds, Exercise 5 first. During Exercise 8, play five against five without goalies with four small goals. During Exercise 5, play one-on-one, with passing receivers. Let the group play on three fields, but change so that Group III changes tasks in the order shown on the right side of the field. After twenty-five minutes players switch exercises.

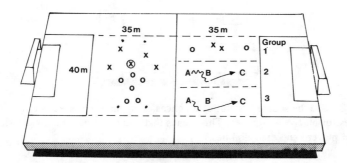

Figure 6.6 *Left half of field*: Using Passing for ten- to fourteen-year-olds, Exercise 8, play five against two plus two goalies. The goals are increased to nine meters. Let one of the two goalies stay in goal when the team attacks. They then play five against two plus one goalie. Change tasks for goalies with regular intervals. *Right half of field*: Using Passing Exercise 5, divide the players into three groups. Group I has four players, Groups II and III have three players each. Groups II and III rotate tasks.

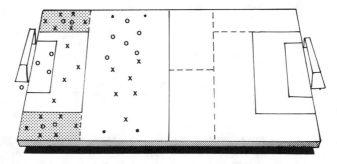

Figure 6.7 Utilize the field's lines as boundaries for practice groups.

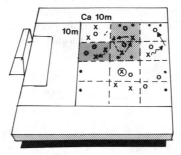

Figure 6.8 Use the square system for practices. You can use one square, two squares, six squares, or all twelve squares. This means that you can match the field's size to the number of players and their abilities.

Part III

Exercises

7

Passing

Passing plays are movements that demonstrate coordination within a team. Through a well-developed passing play you can develop attacks and create goal chances. For this, you must require technical knowledge of the ball handler, and good movement and correct placements of the teammates in relationship to the ball handler. To achieve as effective a passing play as possible, you should, in small team plays, stress the basics of attacking plays.

Many players are not aware of the distance between themselves and the closest teammate when they receive the pass. Therefore, they do not know if they should keep the ball and turn in the attacking direction, or give a direct pass to a teammate. The players must learn to take their eyes away from the ball.

If they always take a glance behind and over the shoulder before they receive a ball, they can decide if they have time enough to control the ball, or if they must play it directly. The player who receives a pass immediately takes over the play initiative.

In attacking play, the most important thing the individual player must understand is how to

- meet the ball and thereby prevent the opposition from breaking up the pass, and
- receive the ball in such a way that it can be kept within the team and a new attack can be started (the player must shield the ball during the entire movement).

Figure 7.1 A passing exercise.

Exercise 1

Passing for seven- to nine-year-olds

Passing Between Players in a Square

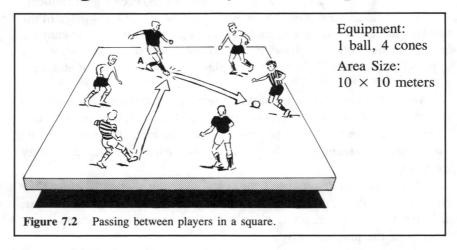

Equipment:
1 ball, 4 cones

Area Size:
10 × 10 meters

Figure 7.2 Passing between players in a square.

Organization
All players are placed at random within the area.

1. Player A starts with a pass to anyone, who controls and immediately passes the ball to another player.
2. Repeat 1, but switch to direct passes (one-touch passes).
3. Player A passes to anyone and follows the ball to the receiver's

spot. The receiver controls the ball, passes as quickly as possible to another player, and follows the ball as A did.

4. Repeat 3, but switch to direct passing (one-touch).

Instructions

Stress the importance of keeping the passes on the ground, making it easier for the receiver. Teach players to stop, control, and pass the ball as quickly as possible, constantly moving toward the ball. By emphasizing ground passes the players can achieve a faster and more accurate passing play.

Passes should gradually become more forceful. Always stress accuracy. The players should always keep the receiver in mind and take their time so they do not miss the receiver. It's important to make sure that all players participate.

Exercise 2	Passing for seven-to-nine-year-olds

Five Against One in a Square

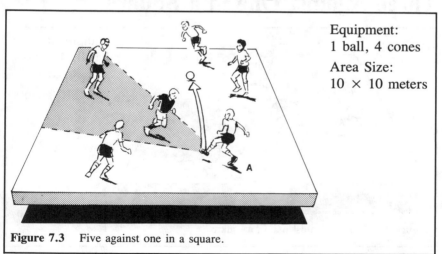

Equipment:
1 ball, 4 cones

Area Size:
10 × 10 meters

Figure 7.3   Five against one in a square.

Organization

Five players move around the area. The one in the middle chases five. The five pass to each other and keep the ball away from the player in the middle.

Let one player try for one minute to get the ball away. Count the number of times he or she touches and/or takes away the ball within that minute. Let all six players play in the middle position. The winner is the player who scores the highest.

Instructions

In this practice you should introduce the concept of the *passing shadow* (see Glossary).

Place a player in front of player A. Then let A explain to the group who is inside and who is outside the passing shadow. Place one player in the shadow and ask what he or she should do to be an effective receiver. Then let everyone stand in the shadow and move out of it to receive a pass. To simplify this exercise in the beginning, you can have the shadowed player walk instead of run.

Exercise 3	Passing for seven- to nine-year-olds

Three Against One in a Square

Equipment:
1 ball, 4 cones

Area Size:
10 × 10 meters

Figure 7.4　Three against one in a square.

Organization

Three players move around the outside boundaries of the square and one player chases them. The three players should pass among themselves so that the one in the middle can't reach the ball.

1. Let one player chase for one minute. Count how many times he or she breaks up the play or touches the ball during this time. Then let the others try to improve on that performance.
2. Vary the setup by changing the player in the middle as soon as he or she breaks up a play and gets control or forces one player to make a bad pass.

Instructions

In conjunction with this exercise, it is suitable to repeat the passing shadow exercise (see Exercise 2). Refer to figures 7.5 through 7.7 for examples of movement patterns with three against one in a square.

Stress the importance of the two passing receivers moving out of the shadow to offer passing alternatives on both sides of the opposing player. To simplify this exercise, in the beginning you can instruct the player in the middle to walk, not run.

Figure 7.5 B and C place themselves far outside of the passing shadow on each side of D. They should not get so close to the ball handler that the play distance becomes too short. The opposing player then reaches the pass receiver before he or she can get control of the ball.

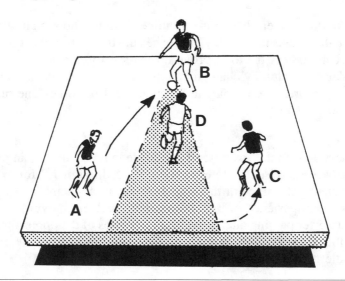

Figure 7.6 A passes to B. D moves and, therefore, the passing shadow moves. C then moves in the direction of the arrow to get out of the shadow and so on.

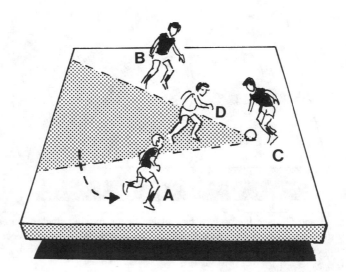

Figure 7.7 B passes to C. D moves, and A takes a new position to get out of the passing shadow.

Exercise 4   Passing for seven- to nine-year-olds

Two Against One Plus One Goalie

Equipment:
1 ball, 8 cones

Area Size:
20 × 10 meters,
2 goals at 5 meters

Figure 7.8   Two against one plus one goalie.

Organization

A and B attack C with D as goalie. After each goalie save, or missed shot, or when C breaks up the play and passes back to goalie D, the attack is over. C and D then attack A with B as goalie.

Note. On the defending team the players should change goalie every other time.

Instructions

The ball handler has two options. Pass to a teammate and take a new position or fake a pass and drive the ball in another direction. Explain how a *passing feint* is done. (See Feints for seven- to nine-year-olds, Exercise 1.) Indicate which of the teammates is avoiding the passing shadow.

If the opposition is pressing the ball handler, the teammate must give support. The ball handler should also, in pressure situations, have the opportunity for a back pass.

Tell your players if the *play distance* is wrong.

One-on-One With Two Pass Receivers

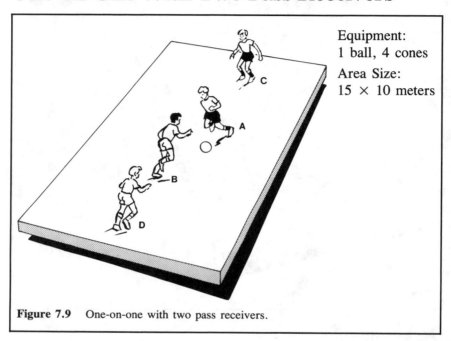

Equipment:
1 ball, 4 cones
Area Size:
15 × 10 meters

Figure 7.9 One-on-one with two pass receivers.

Organization

Player A starts out as ball handler and tries to make a pass to D who moves along the touchline. If A succeeds a point is awarded. A then turns and starts by getting the ball from D and then tries to pass to C. Whenever B breaks up the play, he or she gets the turn to get a pass past A. The players get 1 point for a pass to any player along either touchline. After two minutes A and B exchange duties with C and D.

Instructions

This exercise is more effective if the defender is close to half-field.

It is important that C and D move all the time, getting out of the passing shadow. The ball handler should think about covering the ball whenever the opposition attacks and he or she can't make a pass. Demonstrate how one covers the ball by having the body between the ball and the opposing player.

The *body feint* is very useful for getting by a player when you play one-on-one. (See Feints for seven- to nine-year-olds, Exercise 4.)

<table>
<tr><td>Exercise 6</td><td>Passing for seven- to nine-year-olds</td></tr>
</table>

Three Against One Plus Two Goalies

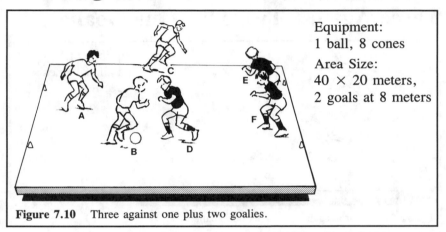

Equipment:
1 ball, 8 cones

Area Size:
40 × 20 meters,
2 goals at 8 meters

Figure 7.10   Three against one plus two goalies.

Organization

A, B, and C attack D who has E and F as goalies. After a goal, save, or miss, or when D breaks up the play and passes back to one of the goalies, the attack is over. D, E, and F then attack A, with B and C as goalies.

Instructions

The ball handler should now have more alternatives. He or she can pass to one of the teammates or fake and go through the defense.

Teammates should concentrate on the ball handler's forward passing possibilities (play depth forward) as well as back support so that he or she can make a back pass whenever the situation arises. The ball handler should not be last in line. The teammates should also learn to avoid the passing shadow.

The three-on-one situation provides a good opportunity to think about not only good depth but also play width. This will help the attack.

There are many ways to guide this practice. You can allow the attackers only two or three touches. Good players can handle one touch. You can also rule that a goal can't be scored until all three attackers have touched the ball.

| Exercise 7 | Passing for seven- to nine-year-olds |

Three Against Two Plus One Goalie

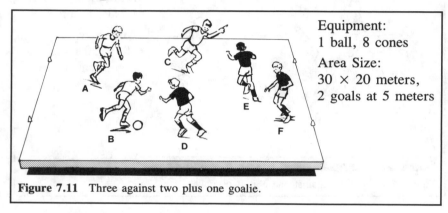

Equipment:
1 ball, 8 cones

Area Size:
30 × 20 meters,
2 goals at 5 meters

Figure 7.11 Three against two plus one goalie.

Organization
A, B, and C play against D and E with F as goalie. A, B, and C will use their numerical advantage to create goal opportunities. After a finished attack, D, E, and F start a new attack against A and B, with C as goalie.

Instructions
The numerical advantage is diminished in this practice. The supporting players (especially the goalie) must give support so that there is a possibility for a back pass.

Exercise 8

Passing for seven- to nine-year-olds

Four Against Two Plus Two Goalies

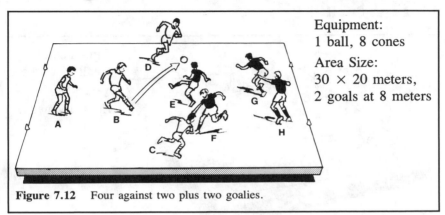

Equipment:
1 ball, 8 cones

Area Size:
30 × 20 meters,
2 goals at 8 meters

Figure 7.12 Four against two plus two goalies.

Organization
A, B, C, and D attack E and F with G and H as goalies. The attack is completed with a goal, goalie save, or miss, or whenever E or F breaks up the play and passes back to either goalie. Then E, F, G, and H attack A and B, with C and D as goalies.

Instructions
The exercise forces players to utilize the basics of attacking play. These have been presented in earlier exercises.

Stress the importance of meeting the ball. Whenever the two outside players of the defending team get the ball, all four players in the attacking team quickly take a defensive position to avoid a back pass to the two goalies. The four attackers can break up such a pass and continue the play as attackers.

It is very common for players to place themselves incorrectly. Many times they break the basic rules of attacking plays. An effective method to remedy this is to freeze the play. Stop the play and tell the players to stay where they are. Then proceed to explain the correct, as well as the incorrect, placements.

There is more information on these methods in chapter 5.

Exercise 1	Passing for ten- to fourteen-year-olds

Six Against Two in a Square ("The Square")

Equipment:
1 ball, 4 cones

Area Size:
15 × 15 meters

Figure 7.13 Six against two in a square ("the square").

Organization

Six players move along the touchlines. These six players pass to each other so that two players chasing the ball cannot break up the play. The six can move along all sides and corners of the square, but cannot change positions among themselves. The players in the middle try to get control of the ball or force one of the six to miss a pass to the outside of the square. It is enough to make a change if one of the defenders just touches the ball. The one who has been in the middle longest changes with the player who either made a missed pass or did not get to the ball in time.

Instructions

In the square, practice a better passing play that creates the ability to play in tighter match-related situations. Even though the situations change with every new pass, there are strict requirements for every player: understanding and individual control in a short time span.

The following basic understandings should be practiced for a good passing play in the square.

1. Play distance. The ball handler should in every situation have the following:
   - Two short passing alternatives. Two players get close to the ball handler, a maximum three meters on each side.
   - At least one long passing alternative. One or more players can be reached with a long pass.
2. Passing shadow. A player in the passing shadow is totally useless to the ball handler. Every new pass forces the teammates of the ball handler to decide whether they are in the passing shadow. If they are, they should move out.
3. Passing feint. The feint is a good method for overtaking an opposing player who is rushing in (e.g., a player who fakes a pass one way and then passes in another direction).
4. Play depth/support.
   - The ball handler should be able to pass the ball a good distance, diagonally or straight across, to a teammate on the other side of the square.
   - The ball handler should have players on each side giving support.
5. The quality of the pass.
   - Keep the ball on the ground.
   - Make the pass easy to receive (i.e., correct speed)
   - Due to pressure from the opposition, make volley and head passes to keep the passing game going.
6. Change between short and long passes. To advance, dare to keep the ball and play many short passes drawing the two in the square closer. Then make a long pass (e.g., short, short, short, long, etc.).
7. Look up. Even before a player receives a pass, he or she should have it clearly in mind where the new pass should go.
8. Talk. The teammates should, in practice as well as the game, give information to each other concerning the play.

With inexperienced players it is recommended to start with two- or three-touch (stop the ball, control, and pass). Your goal should be one-touch. Count the passes until someone in the middle touches the ball.

The square gives practice a game-like passing situation and is very good as a starting exercise for a practice session. After some practice the passing game is bound to improve considerably, but the ultimate result is reached after constant repetition of practices in the square.

Exercise 2   Passing for ten- to fourteen-year-olds

Soccer Tennis

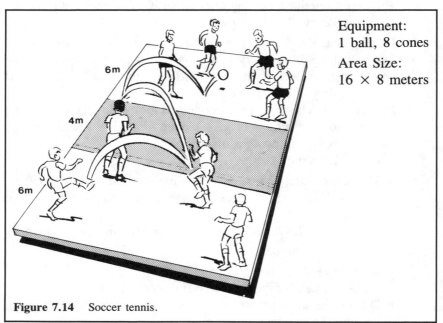

Equipment:
1 ball, 8 cones

Area Size:
16 × 8 meters

Figure 7.14   Soccer tennis.

Organization

Organize two teams of four each. Both sides use an area of 6 x 8 meters. Between them is a no-man's-land, 4 x 8 meters in dimension. The ball is served from the base line and must pass over the no-man's-land.

The ball can bounce one time before it must be returned. The players should have one successful pass in the air before the ball is returned to the other side, and the ball cannot be touched by hand. If the ball bounces outside of the playing areas or in the no-man's-land, the team making the last touch loses a point. Play until one team has 15 points.

Instructions

This practice is excellent for improving volleys and headers. You can make the exercise more difficult by not allowing the ball to touch the ground. If you can get a net, place it in the no-man's-land. This exercise is also good for station practice.

Passing for ten- to fourteen-year-olds

Two Against One in a Square

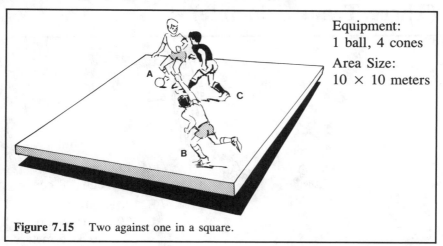

Equipment:
1 ball, 4 cones

Area Size:
10 × 10 meters

Figure 7.15   Two against one in a square.

Organization

A and B will try to get as many passes as possible to each other within the square before C breaks up the play. Whenever C breaks up the play, he or she changes with the player touching the ball last. If the ball goes outside of the square, the player last touching the ball becomes the defender. Compete to see which pair has the highest number of continuous passes.

Instructions

The ball handler should utilize pass feints as an alternative to passes. The teammate gets good practice moving out of the passing shadow. The size of the square can vary. Higher experience level requires a smaller square.

| Exercise 4 | Passing for ten- to fourteen-year-olds |

Two Against One Plus One Goalie (Three Team Principle)

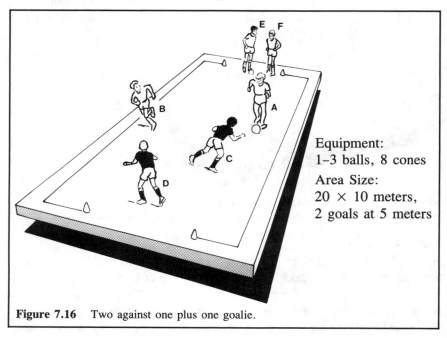

Equipment:
1–3 balls, 8 cones

Area Size:
20 × 10 meters,
2 goals at 5 meters

Figure 7.16   Two against one plus one goalie.

Organization
A and B attack C with D as goalie. After a completed attack, C and D take the ball behind the goal and attack E with F as goalie. At the completion of this attack, E and F take their ball and attack A with B as goalie.

Instructions
One of the advantages of this three team principle is that after an attack the team does not have to rush back to defend its goal. Another team has already taken over the defending duties.

Repeat using pass feints. The ball handler has two options: Pass and move to an open position, or fake a pass and dribble past the opposing player. The ball handler's teammate should always avoid the passing shadow.

Exercise 5   Passing for ten- to fourteen-year-olds

Three Against Two Plus One Goalie

Equipment:
1 ball, 8 cones

Area Size:
30 × 20 meters,
2 goals at 5 meters

Figure 7.17   Three against two plus one goalie.

Organization
A, B, and C are playing against D and E with F as goalie. A, B, and C should utilize their numerical advantage to advance for a shot on goal. After a completed attack, D, E, and F start a new attack against A and B with C as goalie.

Instructions
You can make the play situation more difficult for the attacking team by allowing only two-touch for them. Encourage them to try one-touch.

| Exercise 6 | Passing for ten- to fourteen-year-olds |

One Plus One Play Maker Against One Plus One Goalie

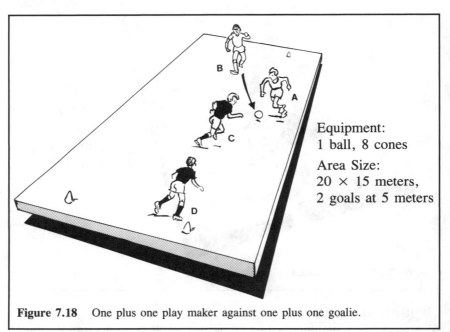

Equipment:
1 ball, 8 cones

Area Size:
20 × 15 meters,
2 goals at 5 meters

Figure 7.18 One plus one play maker against one plus one goalie.

Organization

Player A attacks to the left and is pressed or marked by C on the defending side of A. B supports A and must play to A even though A is marked. A tries to move out of the marking and must decide whether he or she can pass by C and take a shot on D. Rather than take a chance, A should play the ball back to B, keeping the ball within the team (back pass). B, giving support, will pass toward A at all times. Play is directed in such a way that B can't finish. After an attack, B starts from his or her own goal again. The teams change duties after two minutes.

Instructions

The practice goal is to play on a marked player and back pass. The marked player tries to get free. Whenever the receiver gets the pass, he or she must decide if it is better to pass back or go for goal. The ability to decide on a correct solution is very important for a successful passing game. The pass receiver always tries to get free. A must change moves and sometimes try to run in the depth, passing by the defender. You should also practice the correct coordination between B's passing and A's running.

Exercise 7	Passing for ten- to fourteen-year-olds

Three Against Three With Two Extra Players Against Small Goals

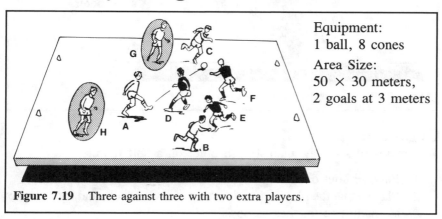

Equipment:
1 ball, 8 cones

Area Size:
50 × 30 meters,
2 goals at 3 meters

Figure 7.19 Three against three with two extra players.

Organization
A, B, and C play against D, E, and F. The neutral players G and H (floaters) belong to the ball handling team but cannot score. The team with the ball plays with a numerical advantage, five against three. Only three-touch is allowed.

Instructions
This exercise stresses playing with confidence and motivates the players to keep the ball within the team because the team that loses the ball is immediately at a numerical disadvantage.

The players should use back passes instead of taking chances with difficult forward passes. The two floaters change sides from the team losing the ball to the team taking over. You can increase the difficulty by allowing only two-touch. Encourage one-touch when it occurs.

Exercise 8   Passing for ten- to fourteen-year-olds

Five Against Five With Goalies

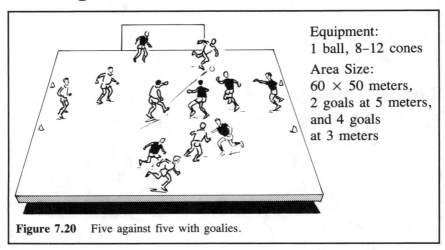

Equipment:
1 ball, 8–12 cones

Area Size:
60 × 50 meters,
2 goals at 5 meters,
and 4 goals
at 3 meters

Figure 7.20   Five against five with goalies.

Organization
Two teams of six play against each other on a half-field.

1. Play without direction.
2. Play so that the players can use three- or two-touch, and try to make as many one-touches as possible.
3. Goals are counted in the normal way. A point is also given for six passes within the team.
4. Play without goalie. Each team has two small goals at the edge of the touch line. This will encourage improving the playing width and squaring off or turning the play.

Instructions
Make sure the players, when practicing, take the opportunity to create goal chances through quickly turning (squaring off) the plays.

Exercise 9

Exercise 9   Passing for ten- to fourteen-year-olds

Six Against Five Plus One Goalie

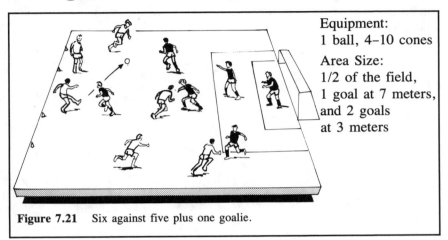

Equipment:
1 ball, 4–10 cones

Area Size:
1/2 of the field,
1 goal at 7 meters,
and 2 goals
at 3 meters

Figure 7.21   Six against five plus one goalie.

Organization

The attacking team has six forwards who play against five players and a goalie. The attacking team tries to score in the large goal and the opposing team scores in the two small goals.

Instructions

In this exercise you can practice set up plays for the defending team. The goals at half-field should be three meters wide. A goal is scored (for the black-shirt team) whenever the ball is passed through the cones and received by a teammate on the other side of the half-field line.

You can make the set-up plays more difficult for the black-shirt team by requiring the receiver across the goal line (midfield line) to pass back to a teammate in the field.

Try to achieve a one-touch pass as often as possible.

Creating Free Play Areas

When closely marked, an attacking player should work very methodically to create free play areas for himself or herself or other teammates. This can be achieved in different ways. See Figures 7.22 through 7.25 for some examples:

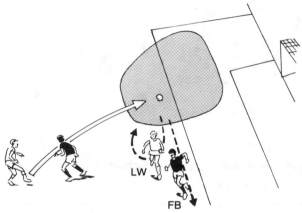

Figure 7.22   The left wing (LW) moves toward the middle and pulls the fullback (FB) with him or her. Suddenly the LW turns back toward the open area that is created on the wing (shaded area).

Figure 7.23   The attacker advances toward the goal, and the marking defender follows. When the attacker suddenly turns and rushes back toward the ball handler and receives the pass, he or she is free from marking and hopefully has enough time to control the ball and turn back toward the goal to challenge the defender.

Figure 7.24 The attacker advances toward the goal. A long pass is played to the marked attacker. This player then passes the ball to the open area that he or she has created. The other attacker can then take over the ball.

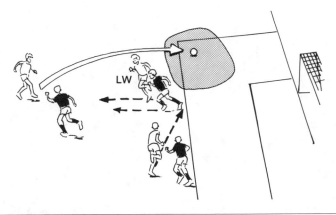

Figure 7.25 The marked LW meets the ball handler, thereby creating a free area on the wing. If another forward or midfield player moves toward that area, he or she can receive the ball behind the LW and the defender. An alternative is to let the LW turn back to the free area. The ball handler then makes a pass down the line passing the oncoming defender.

8

Feints

It often happens in modern soccer that a team has an equal amount of opposing players in one specific area of the field. The ball handler is squeezed into a small area, and all teammates are marked. The players then play one-on-one. They end up in a situation where the only escape is to dribble, which means that the ball handler, with the ball under control, tries to get by an opposing player.

The player often has difficulty succeeding with the dribble if he or she does not execute a *feint* to get the opponent off balance. The ball handler fakes whenever he or she tries to get the opponent to believe that he or she is doing one thing but does something else (e.g., fakes to the right, but actually goes to the left).

The ability to fake is especially valuable in front of the goal. The player can, on his or her own initiative, get free and perhaps score a goal.

Even on other areas of the field, it is important to be able to overtake an opponent. Sometimes it is necessary to keep the ball (fake and dribble) to give teammates time to find open positions. Therefore, every player will need to know at least one feint—preferably a personal feint by which the player can pass by an opposing player and then play on.

Feints take lots of practice. The feint should be a surprising move that allows the ball handler to gain a couple of steps on the opponent. Some of the most common feints are illustrated in Figures 8.1 through 8.5. If you discover a player that does another feint, encourage him or her in all possible ways to develop that feint into a personal specialty.

Faking techniques should be practiced at a very young age and thereafter be improved during the soccer career. The technique with the ball and the movement of a player is quite simple. The difficulty is to do it in a one-on-one situation. Therefore, the time should be spent practicing against opponents. For teaching practicality, only one feint should be practiced at each coaching session.

Shooting Feint

In Figure 8.1a through d, Mike is attacking the goal and is challenged by Ryan. Mike feints a shot and Ryan reacts by reaching with his left foot to stop the ball. Now, Mike has stepped out of balance, and Mike pulls the ball to his left to get closer to the goal.

Mike then should finish his shooting feint with a shot on goal.

Figure 8.1 Shooting Feint.

Heel Feint

In Figure 8.2a through e, Sean is driving the ball forward and he is challenged by John. Suddenly, Sean fakes a heel kick. He steps over the ball with his right foot, moves it back again, and suddenly kicks the ball forward. The feint should always be executed with the foot furthest away from the challenging player.

Figure 8.2 Heel Feint.

Turning Feint

In Figure 8.3a through e, the ball handler is left fullback and is driving the ball toward his own goal. Assume that he is followed by an opposing player. He shows clearly that he intends to play the ball toward his own left. Instead of kicking the ball, he steps over the ball with his right foot and drives it to the right with the outside of his right foot.

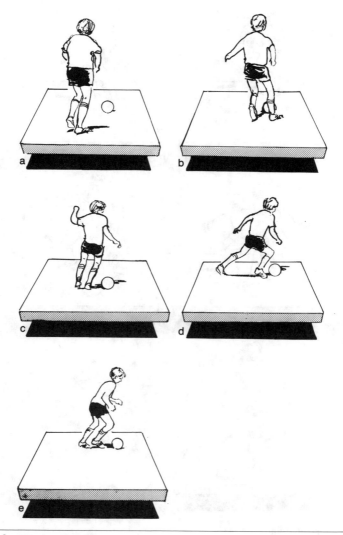

Figure 8.3 Turning Feint.

Passing Feint

In Figure 8.4a through e, the ball handler is driving the ball forward in the attacking direction. Assume that he will be challenged. He then turns his body to the right and fakes a pass to a teammate. Instead of completing the pass, he pulls the ball quickly with the right foot toward the left and passes by the opposing player.

Figure 8.4 Passing Feint.

Body Feint

This feint can be executed in both directions. In Figure 8.5a through e, the ball handler makes some very exaggerated body movements in the direction opposite to which he intends to play the ball. The technique is basically the same for many players, but the execution is purely personal. It is important not only to lift your foot over the ball, but, at all times, to move the body toward the opposite direction.

Figure 8.5 Body Feint.

Exercise 1   Feints for seven- to nine-year-olds

Two Against One Plus One Goalie

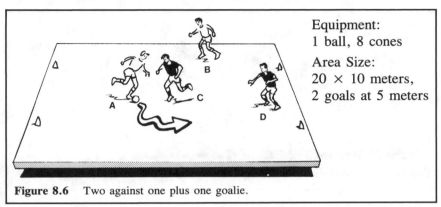

Equipment:
1 ball, 8 cones

Area Size:
20 × 10 meters,
2 goals at 5 meters

Figure 8.6   Two against one plus one goalie.

Organization

A and B attack C with D as goalie. After a goal, goalie save, or miss, or when C gets the ball and plays it back to the goalie D, the play is finished. C and D then attack A with B as goalie.

Note. On the defending team, the players should change their functions every other play.

Instructions

This exercise can be executed in conjunction with a wall pass (see chapter 9, Exercise 1, seven- to nine-year-olds). Here you introduce an alternative to wall play, a passing feint. To make this exercise a feint exercise, you should reward clean feints.

Point system:

- 1 point for a regular goal.
- 1 point for a successful feint.
- 3 points for a feint and a goal.

Whenever the defenders realize that the attacker fakes every time, you can change the point awards:

- 1 point for a regular goal.
- 1 point for a feint and a wall pass.
- 3 points for a feint and a goal or a wall pass and a goal.

| Exercise 2 | Feints for seven- to nine-year-olds |

One-on-One Plus Two Walls

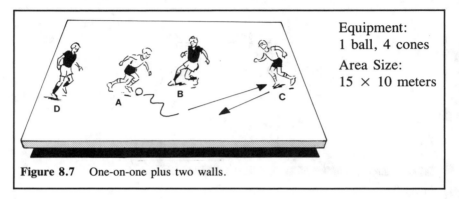

Equipment:
1 ball, 4 cones

Area Size:
15 × 10 meters

Figure 8.7   One-on-one plus two walls.

Organization

A plays against B in the square. A gets points if he or she can fake a wall pass to C (passing feint), but instead dribbles by B and passes to C and gets the ball back. Whenever A is successful he or she turns around toward D. If B gets the ball, he or she repeats the exercise same as A.

After a minute the players change tasks so that C and D do the faking. A and B become the backboards who can move only on the line between the cones.

Instructions

Playing one-on-one provides an excellent opportunity to practice feints. With this setup the passing feint becomes most popular if you combine the exercise with a wall pass.

Exercise 3   Feints for seven- to nine-year-olds

Two Against One Plus One Goalie

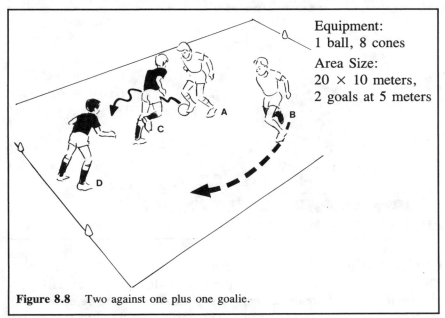

Equipment:
1 ball, 8 cones

Area Size:
20 × 10 meters,
2 goals at 5 meters

Figure 8.8   Two against one plus one goalie.

Organization
A and B attack C with D as goalie. The attack is finished whenever a goal is saved or scored, or a shot misses the goal, or C breaks up the play and passes back to goalie D. C and D then attack A with B as goalie.

Instructions
The exercise can be combined with overlapping (see chapter 11) which you can alternate with a passing feint.

Point System:

- 1 point for a regular goal.
- 1 point for a successful overlapping or a passing feint.
- 3 points for overlapping plus a goal or a passing feint plus a goal.

Feints for seven- to nine-year-olds

Passing Feint–Shoot

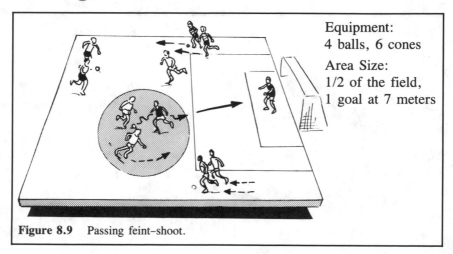

Equipment:
4 balls, 6 cones

Area Size:
1/2 of the field,
1 goal at 7 meters

Figure 8.9   Passing feint–shoot.

Organization

The players start in groups of two from the midfield. A defender is just outside the penalty area. The ball handler challenges the defender, and the teammate moves to open spots. The purpose of the drill is to score goals. When the defenders have made three attempts, they switch with an attacking team. Goalies will change after three attacks.

Instructions

If you combine this drill with overlapping (chapter 11), the ball handler has the option of passing to an overlapping player or making a passing feint and dribbling past the defender.

| Exercise 5 | Feints for seven- to nine-year-olds |

One-on-One Against One Goalie

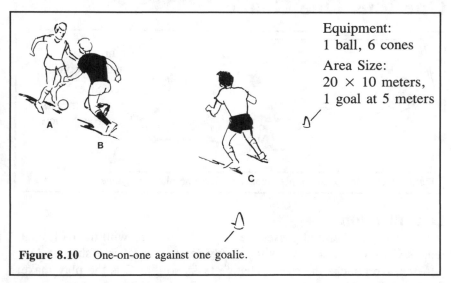

Equipment:
1 ball, 6 cones

Area Size:
20 × 10 meters,
1 goal at 5 meters

Figure 8.10   One-on-one against one goalie.

Organization
A and B play against each other, each trying to score on C. After one minute the tasks are changed so that B plays against C and A is goalie.

Instructions
Some of the players will try to execute something looking like a *body feint*. Stop the play, gather the players, let the player who faked repeat the move, and give praise. Tell the players that the move is called a body feint and show it once more at a slower pace.

Let the players go back to their groups and direct them to do the feint by awarding a point for every body feint and goal.

Exercise 6 | Feints for seven- to nine-year-olds

One Plus One Play Maker Against One Plus One Goalie

Equipment:
1 ball, 6 cones
Area Size:
20 × 10 meters,
1 goal at 5 meters

Figure 8.11 One plus one play maker against one plus one goalie.

Organization

A is the play maker and passes the ball to B. B turns with the ball, challenges C by trying to fake with a body feint, and takes a shot on D.

After five attacks the teams change tasks so that C is the play maker for D, A is goalie, and B is defender.

Instructions

If C, who starts from the touchline, reaches B, who starts at the middle of the square, before B gets control of the ball and has a chance to turn toward the goal, then the ball must be played back to the play maker A and the attack starts again. B must have a chance to turn into the attacking direction and execute a feint. Therefore, B is forced to meet the ball.

| Exercise 7 | Feints for seven- to nine-year-olds |

Receive/Break Through One Defender Plus One Goalie

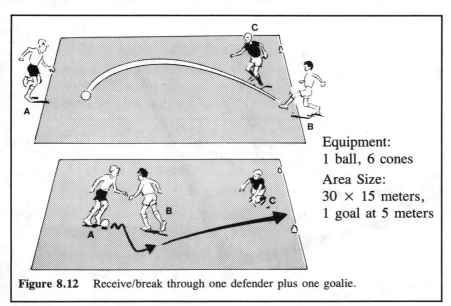

Equipment:
1 ball, 6 cones

Area Size:
30 × 15 meters,
1 goal at 5 meters

Figure 8.12   Receive/break through one defender plus one goalie.

Organization
B plays a high kick to A from the touchline. C is the goalie. A controls the ball and advances toward the goal. B is the defender. A fakes and tries to get past B to score.

After five tries the players change positions so that A becomes goalie, B attacker, and C defender.

Instructions
Some of the players will use the *shooting feint*. When this happens, stop the practice, let the player show how it's done, praise the player, and let all know that the move is called a shooting feint.

Let the players go back to practicing both the body feint and the shooting feint in one-on-one situations.

Exercise 8

Three Against Two Plus One Goalie

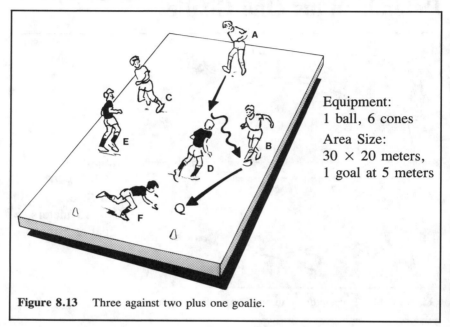

Equipment:
1 ball, 6 cones

Area Size:
30 × 20 meters,
1 goal at 5 meters

Figure 8.13   Three against two plus one goalie.

Organization

A, B, and C attack D and E with F as goalie. After a completed attack, D, E, and F start a new attack against A and B with C as goalie.

Note. All players should play goalie at least one time.

Instructions

In a situation with three attackers against two defenders there are excellent opportunities for feints.

Exercise 1   Feints for ten- to fourteen-year-olds

Play to Own Goalie

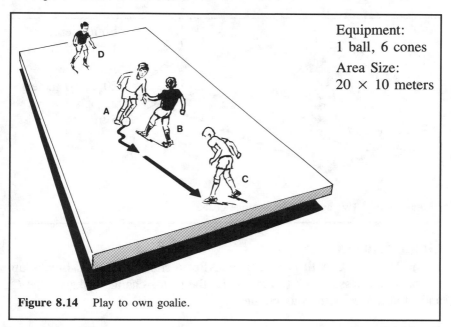

Equipment:
1 ball, 6 cones

Area Size:
20 × 10 meters

Figure 8.14   Play to own goalie.

Organization

A plays against B and tries to reach C with a pass. If A succeeds, A will continue with the ball trying to play the ball to D. If B breaks up the play, B gets the chance to play back to C and D, who remain at the cones. After a minute, the players change so that C and D play against each other. A and B become goalie targets.

Instructions

Use this exercise to reinforce the body feint. It is also an improvement drill for players who have developed their own personal feint.

| Exercise 2 | Feints for ten- to fourteen-year-olds |

Two Against One Plus One Goalie

Equipment:
1 ball, 8 cones

Area Size:
20 × 10 meters,
2 goals at
5 meters

Figure 8.15   Two against one plus one goalie.

Organization

A and B attack C with D as goalie. After a shot or when C breaks up the play and passes back to the goalie, the teams change tasks so that C and D attack A with B as goalie.

Instructions

You can combine the exercise with leaving (see chapter 10). The defender in this exercise soon will notice that the ball handler A passes the ball every time to teammate B. The defender can then concentrate on what B will do when he or she gets the ball. Some players will find out that it pays off for the ballhandler to fake a pass and keep the ball and try to finish the attack. A *heel feint* will increase the effectiveness of the *fake leave*.

Faking the leave, executed with a heel feint, is then an alternative to the leave.

Point system:

- 1 point for a regular goal.
- 1 point for a successful leave or a fake leave plus a heel feint.
- 3 points for leaving plus a goal or fake leave plus a heel feint plus a goal.

Exercise 3   Feints for ten- to fourteen-year-olds

One Plus Three Against Three Plus One Goalie

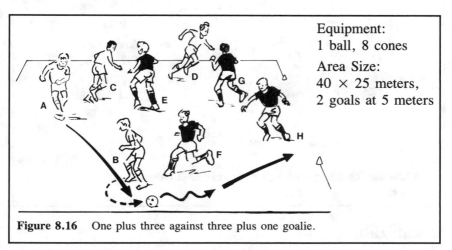

Equipment:
1 ball, 8 cones

Area Size:
40 × 25 meters,
2 goals at 5 meters

Figure 8.16 One plus three against three plus one goalie.

Organization

A, B, C, and D attack E, F, and G with H as goalie. A should only give support and never be in front of B, C, or D.

After a finished attack the defenders change with the attackers.

Instructions

A, who gives support, can create situations for some teammates to make a *turning feint* and surprisingly start an attack on the goal.

| Exercise 4 | Feints for ten- to fourteen-year-olds |

Six Against Five Plus One Goalie

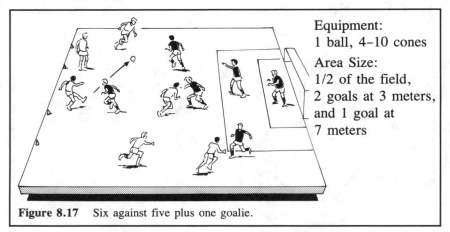

Equipment:
1 ball, 4–10 cones

Area Size:
1/2 of the field,
2 goals at 3 meters,
and 1 goal at
7 meters

Figure 8.17   Six against five plus one goalie.

Organization

The white-shirt team, with six players, attacks the black-shirt team with five players and a goalie.

The attacking team tries to score in the large goal whereas the defenders try to score in one of two small goals at midfield.

Instructions

The players have now learned and had the opportunity to practice some feints. In one-on-one situations they have practiced body and shot feints. In two-on-one situations they have practiced pass-heel and turn feints. Now it's time to see if the players can use their acquired skills. Direct this exercise toward a feint play.

Point system:

- 1 point for any basic feint or any self-developed feint.
- 1 point for a goal.
- 3 points for a goal after a feint.

9 ⚽ Wall Play

lways emphasize attacking plays in soccer practices. Stress the importance of achieving a numerical advantage. The players should try to outnumber the opponent two against one. In that way they have a better chance to outplay one defender and advance to the goal.

The wall play is an attacking method. Even at the start of an attack the wall play is helpful. Its most important advantage is in the conclusion of an attack when one tries to get through a strong defense.

In a basic approach to the wall play, the ball handler is in a two-on-one situation challenging the opposing player. Then he or she passes to a teammate, the wall, who is free on one side, and rushes quickly past the defender. The wall's job is to pass the ball in front of the ball handler (Figure 9.1).

Figure 9.1 Wall play.

The closer you get to the defending goal the more difficult it is to create a two-on-one situation. To be successful in these wall plays, the attackers must be willing to play on marked players. A wall player must be able to play with a defender on his or her back.

Figure 9.2 Play on marked players.

An additional development of the wall play is the double pass. This is like two wall passes in a row. The ball handler makes a wall pass, rushes up, and gets the ball back. As soon as the wall plays the ball, he or she turns and rushes in the direction of the attack and receives a pass from the original ball handler. The first time the ball handler must play straight on against the defender. The second time he or she must play in the defender's direction (Figure 9.3).

A successful combination requires good timing between the players. Only through constant repetition at practice sessions can good execution be realized in the game. Many factors must be incorporated for a successful wall play.

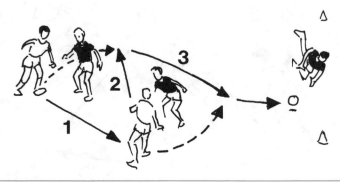

Figure 9.3 Double pass.

The Ball Handler's Role

The ball handler must accomplish the following tasks (see Figure 9.4).

- Change tempo from a slow pace before the pass to a quicker pace just after the pass.
- Challenge the opposing player before the pass is made.
- Conceal the wall pass so that it surprises the opposition.
- Do not pass too early, or the opposition will have time to turn.
- Do not execute the pass too late, or the opposition will come too close.
- Make the direction of the pass straight to the wall (the teammate) and adjust the power of the pass to the distance.
- Time the speed of the rush and the power of the pass.

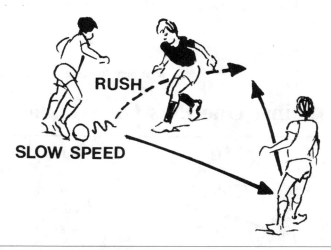

Figure 9.4   The ball handler's movement:

1. Challenge (be aware of dribbling alternatives).
2. Hit the pass straight on the wall.
3. Change tempo. Rush!

The Wall's Role

The wall must be placed outside of the passing shadow; dare to remain a wall, even if he or she is marked, and meet the ball whenever the pass comes so that he or she reaches the ball before the opposing player; and play the ball directly or with delay in the direction of the receiver (see Figure 9.5).

Figure 9.5 The wall's movement:

1. Move out of the passing shadow.
2. Dare to remain the wall even though marked.
3. Play the ball back to the ball handler, either directly or with delay.

| Exercise 1 | Wall play for seven- to nine-year-olds |

Two Against One Plus One Goalie

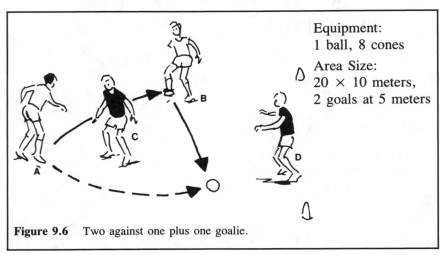

Equipment:
1 ball, 8 cones

Area Size:
20 × 10 meters,
2 goals at 5 meters

Figure 9.6 Two against one plus one goalie.

Organization

A and B attack C with D as goalie. After a goal, goalie save, or shot outside of goal, or when C breaks up the play and passes back to goalie D, the play is over. C and D then attack A with B as goalie.

Note. The players change tasks every other attack in the defending team.

Instructions

At the start of the drill, it is possible that the players will attack in a line. This is not correct. They do not gain any ground with a pass. If the defender breaks up the play, both attackers are out of the play (see Figure 9.7).

Figure 9.7 Here player A should have executed a better challenge.

Your task is to observe and note as soon as one player executes something looking like a wall play.

- Freeze the situation.
- Gather all players and let those who made the wall play do it again.
- Praise.
- Explain that the method is called a wall play and that it is very effective in attacking plays.

Let the players show the move one more time slowly and explain all moves (refer to Figure 9.6):

1. A challenges C.
2. B is placed in the depth behind C, turning toward A (not in the passing shadow).
3. A passes the ball straight to B and rushes on the other side of C.
4. B passes the ball directly into A's path of movement.
5. A tries to score a goal.

To motivate the players, direct the play toward many wall play attempts.

Point System:

- 1 point for a regular goal.
- 1 point for a successful wall play.
- 3 points for a wall play plus a goal.

After a time the defenders will discover that it pays to cut off the passing options of a wall play. It is then time to introduce alternatives to a wall pass.

The best alternative is perhaps a *pass feint* (see chapter 8). Instead of making a difficult pass to the wall, the ball handler fakes the pass and goes past the defender on the other side. Such a feint should be rewarded as highly as a wall play.

Point System:

- 1 point for a regular goal.
- 1 point for a successful wall play.
- 1 point for a correctly executed pass feint.
- 3 points for a wall play plus a goal.
- 3 points for a pass feint plus a goal.

| Exercise 2 | Wall play for seven- to nine-year-olds |

One-on-One With Two Walls

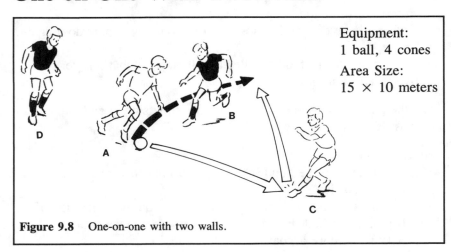

Equipment:
1 ball, 4 cones

Area Size:
15 × 10 meters

Figure 9.8   One-on-one with two walls.

Organization

A plays against B within the square. A gets 1 point if he or she can play the ball to C, and receive the pass back immediately (wall play). If A is successful, he or she must at once play to D using a wall pass. If B breaks up the pass, he or she has a chance for points in the same manner as A.

After one minute, the players change tasks so that C and D play against each other. A and B become walls.

Instructions

If the wall in the previous exercise (Exercise 1) has problems positioning in depth, you may use this exercise. Here the wall is always behind the defender and has only one task: to get out of the passing shadow and get open for a pass.

There is the risk in this drill that the defender will be more interested in blocking the wall plays than attacking the ball handler. Let the ball handler fake and dribble, and reward the feint and the pass with high scores.

Exercise 3	Wall play for seven- to nine-year-olds

Two Against One Plus One Goalie

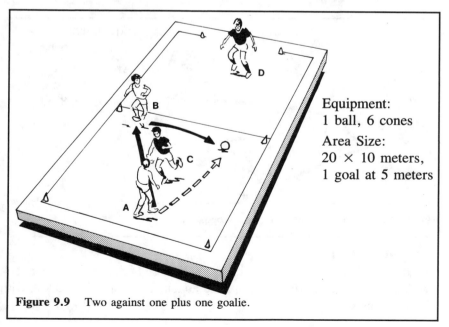

Equipment:
1 ball, 6 cones

Area Size:
20 × 10 meters,
1 goal at 5 meters

Figure 9.9   Two against one plus one goalie.

Organization

A and B start out with a ball behind the cones that are farthest from the goal. C starts between the cones at midfield and challenges the ball handler. A plays a wall pass to B or feints past C.

After five attacks the teams change positions so that C and D attack. A is goalie and B defends.

Note. The players change goalie tasks after a completed exercise.

Instructions

The wall play is now at the most important stage—action closest to the goal. If B has problems working within the square, move him or her outside, keeping both A and C within the square.

In addition, to create a two-on-one situation through a wall play or passing feint, a third alternative is to let the wall turn up and finish the attack. The team scoring the most goals in ten attacks is the winner.

| Exercise 4 | Wall play for seven- to nine-year-olds |

Three Against One Plus Two Goalies

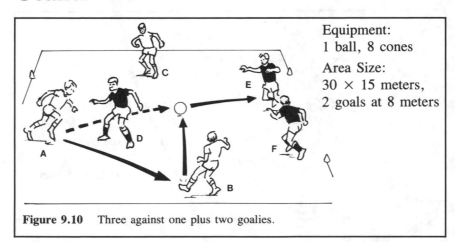

Equipment:
1 ball, 8 cones

Area Size:
30 × 15 meters,
2 goals at 8 meters

Figure 9.10　Three against one plus two goalies.

Organization

A, B, and C attack D with E and F as goalies. Only A can finish an attack with a shot on goal. After a completed attack, D, E, and F attack A with B and C as goalies.

The defending teams change field player every turn. The attackers change finishing player at the same time.

Instructions

The attacking team now has three players against one. After practicing with two against one earlier, one can assume that the wall play gets easier. In the beginning, however, the ball handler will have problems executing a pass at the correct time, depending on what influence the extra player applies. The ball handler is in a selecting position and may become confused.

After a time, the wall play will flow again with more improvements. We have two wall play alternatives in most cases. The players can now concentrate on wall plays and do not have to think about pass feints.

Whenever the players become proficient, you should introduce the passing feint again.

Point System:

- 1 point for a regular goal.
- 1 point for a wall pass or a pass feint.
- 3 points for a wall pass and a goal, or a pass feint and a goal.

| Exercise 5 | Wall play for seven- to nine-year-olds |

Three Against Two Plus One Goalie

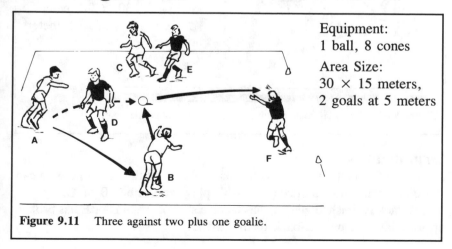

Equipment:
1 ball, 8 cones

Area Size:
30 × 15 meters,
2 goals at 5 meters

Figure 9.11   Three against two plus one goalie.

Organization

A, B, and C attack D and E with F as goalie. After a completed attack, D, E, and F start an attack against A and B with C as goalie.

Note. The defending team changes goalie after every attack.

Instructions

The ball handler now has two pass alternatives and two opposing players. It becomes more difficult for the players to find wall play situations. Because you are directing the play, encourage the players to try to succeed.

Point System:

- 1 point for a regular goal.
- 1 point for a wall play.
- 3 points for a wall play and a goal.

Exercise 6	Wall play for seven- to nine-year-olds

One Play Maker Plus Two Against Two Plus One Goalie

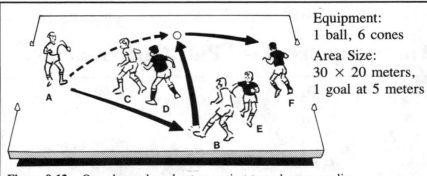

Equipment:
1 ball, 6 cones

Area Size:
30 × 20 meters,
1 goal at 5 meters

Figure 9.12   One play maker plus two against two plus one goalie.

Organization

A, B, and C attack D and E with F as goalie. A is the only one who can score and only after a successful wall play with either B or C.

An attack is finished when A has taken a shot or when D or E has broken up the play and passed back to the goalie.

After five attacks the teams change tasks so that D, E, and F attack B and C with A as goalie.

All players in the defense should rotate as goalie. The attacking team should also rotate the player finishing the attack.

Instructions

This exercise provides many opportunities for wall plays. There are also fine opportunities for feints. At this stage, it is appropriate to introduce the *shooting feint*.

| Exercise 1 | Wall play for ten- to fourteen-year-olds |

Two Against One Plus One Goalie (Three Team Principle)

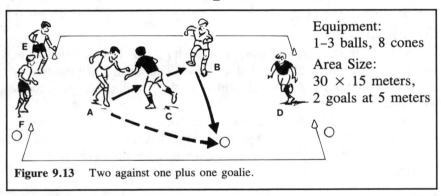

Equipment:
1–3 balls, 8 cones

Area Size:
30 × 15 meters,
2 goals at 5 meters

Figure 9.13 Two against one plus one goalie.

Organization

A and B attack C with D as goalie. After a finished attack, C and D take their ball from behind the goal and attack E with F as goalie. A and B get their ball at the same time and wait at the right side goal. After a completed attack, E and F take their ball and attack A with B as goalie. Whenever A and B take a shot, or whenever C breaks up the play and passes back to D, C and D start an attack against E with F as goalie.

Instructions

The benefit of playing two against one plus goalie with the three team principle is that the attacking team does not have to rush back after a completed attack. A third team takes over the defending duties whenever C and D go to the attack.

Exercise 2	Wall play for ten- to fourteen-year-olds

Four Against Three Plus One Goalie (Three Team Principle)

Equipment:
1–3 balls, 8 cones

Area Size:
40 × 20 meters,
2 goals at 5 meters

Figure 9.14   Four against three plus one goalie.

Organization

The white-shirt team has four field players who attack the black-shirt team, which has three field players and a goalie. The attacking team tries to create two-on-one situations and, with the help of wall plays, get past the opposition.

After a successful attack the black-shirt team starts a new attack with four players against the striped-shirt team that has three field players and a goalie. Next time, the striped-shirt team attacks the white-shirt team. Continue rotation.

Instructions

As you notice, the requirement of the players is now a higher performance level. With four field players against three it is more difficult to create goal chances than with two against one.

Point System:

- 1 point for each goal.
- 1 point for a successful wall play.
- 3 points for a wall play plus a goal.

Exercise 3   Wall play for ten- to fourteen-year-olds

One Play Maker Plus Three Against Three Plus One Goalie

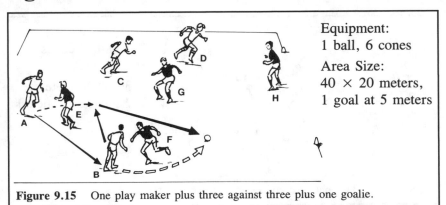

Equipment:
1 ball, 6 cones

Area Size:
40 × 20 meters,
1 goal at 5 meters

Figure 9.15   One play maker plus three against three plus one goalie.

Organization
A, B, C, and D attack E, F, and G with H as goalie. A is the setup player and can also take part in the finish if he or she has been able to make a wall play with B, C, or D.

After three attacks, the teams change tasks.

Instructions
In this exercise there are opportunities for the players to try a double wall pass. Whenever this happens

- freeze the play,
- gather all participants,
- let the players execute again,
- praise, and
- explain that it's called a double pass.

Finally, show the double pass again and comment on every detail. This exercise is also suitable for feint exercises.

Point System:

- 1 point for a goal.
- 2 points for every double pass (the double pass is very difficult and should get a high score).
- 4 points for a double pass and a goal.

| Exercise 4 | Wall play for ten- to fourteen-year-olds |

Two Plus Two Goalies Against Two Plus Two Goalies

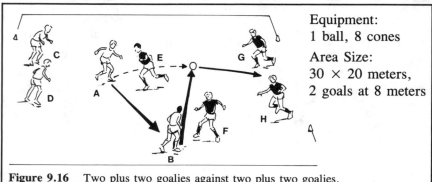

Equipment:
1 ball, 8 cones

Area Size:
30 × 20 meters,
2 goals at 8 meters

Figure 9.16 Two plus two goalies against two plus two goalies.

Organization
A and B with goalies C and D play against E and F with goalies G and H. After two minutes, the players change tasks so that G and H with goalies E and F attack C and D with goalies A and B.

Instructions
The attacking and defending teams have the same number of players. Opportunities for wall plays are now limited. Therefore, you should try to guide players toward wall plays.

This exercise is suitable for feint coaching. Some players should try the heel feint. Take the opportunity to introduce it.

Point System:
- 1 point for a goal.
- 1 point for a wall pass.
- 3 points for a wall pass plus a goal.

Exercise 5

Three Against Three

Equipment:
1 ball, 8 cones

Area Size:
30 × 20 meters

Figure 9.17 Three against three.

Organization
A, B, and C play against D, E, and F. Time: Three minutes play, three minutes rest. Three repetitions.

Instructions
Because it is difficult to get wall plays going with three against three, you must encourage every attempt. Direct the play so that the players will try wall plays.

Point System:
- 1 point for a regular goal.
- 1 point for a successful wall pass.
- 3 points for a wall pass and a goal.

| Exercise 6 | Wall play for ten- to fourteen-year-olds |

Six Against Five Plus One Goalie

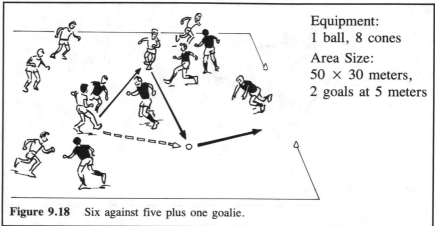

Equipment:
1 ball, 8 cones
Area Size:
50 × 30 meters,
2 goals at 5 meters

Figure 9.18 Six against five plus one goalie.

Organization

Six attackers on the white-shirt team attack five forwards and a goalie on the black-shirt team.

After an attack is concluded, the teams change tasks.

Instructions

Continue to encourage all wall passes. Use the same scoring methods that were used earlier.

Point System:

- 1 point for a regular goal.
- 1 point for a successful wall pass.
- 3 points for a wall pass and a goal.

Exercise 7   Wall play for ten- to fourteen-year-olds

Six Against Five Plus One Goalie; One Goal and Two Small Goals

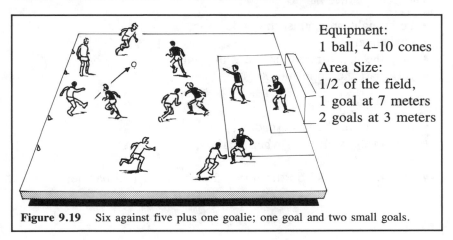

Equipment:
1 ball, 4–10 cones

Area Size:
1/2 of the field,
1 goal at 7 meters
2 goals at 3 meters

Figure 9.19   Six against five plus one goalie; one goal and two small goals.

Organization
The white-shirt team that attacks has six forwards playing against the black-shirt team that has five forwards and one goalie.

Instructions
In the beginning, only the three front line players on the white-shirt team can score. Direct the midfield players to act only as play makers. However, a player succeeding with a wall pass may advance and take a shot on goal.

It is also important to slowly and methodically build up the attack. The best situation occurs when all midfield players are able to finish an attack.

The black-shirt team will score in one of the small goals in midfield. The main task for the black-shirt team is to change over to attack whenever they get the ball and not to think only defense. The goalie also attacks by throwing the ball toward the sides to some of the outside backs. They should get used to attacking when they get the ball and a good attacking situation is created.

By now the players should be proficient enough in wall plays so that you may apply restrictions. They should be ready to find different wall play techniques and even select the ones most suitable for the team.

As a coach you should also try to instruct and correct every detail to achieve the best wall plays possible.

The ball handler has to

- go straight on against the opposition,
- challenge,
- play the ball directly on the wall, and
- rush past the opposition.

The wall has to

- move out of the pass shadow,
- remain the wall even when marked,
- meet the ball, and
- pass the ball back in the forward path of the ball handler.

10 ⚽

Leaving

L eaving is used in attacking plays to

- turn the play,
- get away from pressing and marking opposition, and
- create tempo (speed) changes in the play.

Leaving takes place between two players whenever a ball handler is driving the ball and a teammate takes over the role as ball handler.

There are two factors that make cooperation an important phase in leaving. This method of attack contradicts the principle of proper play distance, and both the ball handler and the teammate can take initiative depending upon the situation. The teammate will have the best opportunity to initiate the leaving because the ball handler might be pressed by the opposition and, therefore, forced to concentrate on other moves.

In the following exercises, these three instructions should be the basics for the ball handler when leaving:

1. Position yourself between opposing player and the ball.
2. Let the ball roll toward the new ball handler—do not pass or stop the ball.
3. Drive the ball with one foot—the foot furthest from the opposing player.

Correctly executed, leaving creates problems for the pressing opposing player because he or she follows the ball toward the direction from which the new ball handler comes. The opposing player therefore has difficulty in quickly turning and pressing the new ball handler.

As an alternative, the ball handler can, through a wall feint just before the leaving, cancel the leaving, and continue with the ball instead.

The situations in which leaving can be most effective occur in the following areas of the field:

- In the midfield, leaving can take place both sideways as well as in depth, mostly to turn the play, but also to avoid marking and to create a change in tempo.
- On the opposing team's half of the field where tight situations develop, leaving, in field depth, is a solution (see Figure 10.1).
- In the penalty area, leaving sideways can create the opportunity to break through or shoot on goal (see Figure 10.2).

Figure 10.1 Leaving in field depth.

Figure 10.2 Leaving sideways.

| Exercise 1 | Leaving for seven- to nine-year-olds |

Number Ball One

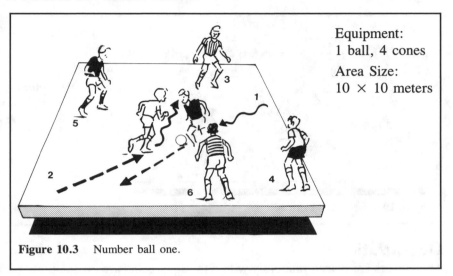

Equipment:
1 ball, 4 cones

Area Size:
10 × 10 meters

Figure 10.3 Number ball one.

Organization

The players are positioned within the square and are given numbers 1 to 6. All should be placed according to the positions shown in Figure 10.3.

Player 1 drives the ball toward 2. Player 2 starts running at the same time toward 1. They meet halfway and the ball handler (1), leaves the ball to 2, who drives the ball toward 1's starting point. From there, 2 starts in the direction toward 3, and so on.

Instructions

The ball handler drives the ball forward with the right foot and leaves the ball first on the right side. Change so the leaving also takes place on the left side. The ball handler lets the ball roll toward the teammate without passing it. The ball handler and teammate should have eye contact to avoid collisions. The ball handler should try to drive the ball without looking down on it.

| Exercise 2 | Leaving for seven- to nine-year-olds |

Number Ball Two

Equipment:
1 ball, 4 cones

Area Size:
10 × 10 meters

Figure 10.4   Number ball two.

Organization

The players are placed randomly within the square and are given numbers 1 to 6. The ball handler (1), looks for 2 and drives the ball toward him or her. At the same time, 2 starts running toward 1, and the leaving takes place. Player 2 then drives the ball toward 3, and so on.

Instructions

The players should always move within the square—even if they are not actively involved in the leaving. Stress the importance of eye contact. The ball handler determines on which side the leaving should take place by driving the ball with the right or left foot.

| Exercise 3 | Leaving for seven- to nine-year-olds |

Leaving Sideways

Equipment:
1 ball, 6 cones

Area Size:
20 × 15 meters,
1 goal

Figure 10.5   Leaving sideways.

Organization
A and B stand in a column as do C and D. B, the ball handler, drives the ball toward D. D runs to meet B halfway to execute the leaving. Whenever D gets the ball from B, he or she drives the ball toward A, who then becomes a ball handler. A and C then execute the same exercise.

Instructions
Determine the direction of the attack. Stress the importance of leaving the ball on the correct side (i.e., the ball handler is between the goal and the ball). Stress that this is called leaving sideways and that it should be executed on the opposing team's half of the field.

As an alternative, let the ball handler fake the leaving, keep the ball, and drive it forward.

Exercise 4   Leaving for seven- to nine-year-olds

Two Against One Plus One Goalie

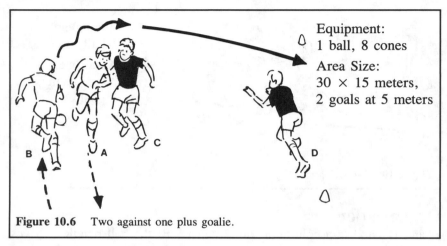

Equipment:
1 ball, 8 cones
Area Size:
30 × 15 meters,
2 goals at 5 meters

B   A   C   D

Figure 10.6   Two against one plus goalie.

Organization

A and B attack C, who has D as goalie. A drives the ball toward B who runs toward A. A lets the ball roll toward B who takes it with him or her, pulls past C, and shoots on D.

If C breaks up the play and passes to the goalie, C and D attack B with A as goalie. At breakups the ball is always passed back to the goalie.

If C turns and follows B, A and B may then turn toward each other and a new leaving situation is created with B as the ball handler. Consequently, B can fake the leaving and keep the ball. The heel feint can be used to increase the effectiveness of the fake leaving.

Instructions

The ball handler should be between the opposing player and the ball at the time of leaving. The exercise should start at a slow pace, the teammates moving relatively slowly toward each other. Whenever the actual leaving takes place, the pace should increase with the new ball handler rushing toward the area vacated by the teammate and opposing player.

Exercise 1   Leaving for ten- to fourteen-year-olds

Three Against Three

Equipment:
1 ball, 4 cones

Area Size:
15 × 15 meters

Figure 10.7   Three against three.

Organization
Play three against three within a restricted area. Leaving should occur here as a complement to the passing play with no specific attack direction. Leaving can be done in all directions in depth as well as sideways.

Instructions
Freeze situations that lend themselves to leaving, especially tight situations in which the ball handler is close to the sideline of the square.

Leaving for ten- to fourteen-year-olds

Four Against Three Plus One Goalie

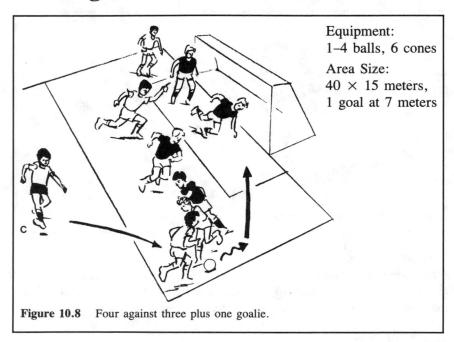

Equipment:
1–4 balls, 6 cones

Area Size:
40 × 15 meters,
1 goal at 7 meters

Figure 10.8   Four against three plus one goalie.

Organization

The coach (C) plays the ball to the attacking team. After executing a leave, the attackers should take a shot on goal as quickly as possible. They cannot shoot in the goal area. The three defenders should try to break up the play or avert a shot. When they get the ball, they play it back to the coach.

Count the goals scored in three minutes, and then change the teams. Both before and after the leave, many passes can be played before a shot on goal is taken.

Instructions

In this exercise, leaving can be practiced both sideways and in depth. Notice the good leaves, and praise the players.

Exercise 3	Leaving for ten- to fourteen-year-olds

Four Against Two Plus Two Goalies

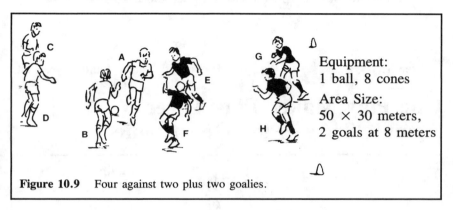

Equipment:
1 ball, 8 cones
Area Size:
50 × 30 meters,
2 goals at 8 meters

Figure 10.9   Four against two plus two goalies.

Organization

A, B, C, and D play against E and F with G and H as goalies. C and D will act as support to A and B by being playable behind A and B. Whenever A and B have executed a leave, the ball can be played to C or D who can shoot against goal or play up again to A or B. A shot on goal may come only after a leave.

Instructions

Let the two defending players mark and follow one attacker each. They should be goal-side (i.e., between the attacker and their own goal). The attacking team starts the attack with lay-ups from one of the supporting players. Stress that eye contact is very important.

Let the teams change tasks whenever E and F break up the play and play back to their goalie, or whenever the play ends with a shot on goal.

Point System:

- 1 point for leaving.
- 2 points for leaving and a shot on goal.
- 3 points for leaving plus a shot on goal and a goal.

Exercise 4	Leaving for ten- to fourteen-year-olds

One Play Maker Plus Three Against Three Plus One Goalie

Equipment:
1 ball, 8 cones

Area Size:
50 × 30 meters,
2 goals at 5 meters

Figure 10.10 One play maker plus three against three plus one goalie.

Organization

The attacking team plays with four players, the rear player being a lay-up player and supporter for the forward. The lay-up player starts with a pass to one of the marked teammates who can either play back or execute a leave sideways with a forward, or in depth with the lay-up player. After the leave, the lay-up player can move in front of the forward and create a shot on goal. Let the players change tasks after five minutes. Count the goals.

Instructions

The lay-up player functions as supporter to the teammates and at all times moves sideways and stays behind them. The players should play back passes if there is no chance for a leave. You may change the lay-up player through a leave or after a finished attack.

Exercise 5	Leaving for ten- to fourteen-year-olds

Six Against Five Plus One Goalie

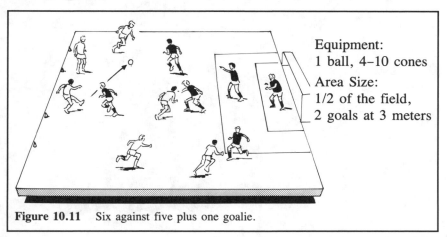

Equipment:
1 ball, 4–10 cones

Area Size:
1/2 of the field,
2 goals at 3 meters

Figure 10.11   Six against five plus one goalie.

Organization
The white-shirt team, with six forwards, attacks the black-shirt team with five players and a goalie. The white-shirt team tries to score in the large goal and the black-shirt team tries to score in the two small goals.

Instructions
The players should try to execute as many leaves as possible. Stress that leaving is an attacking tactic that should take place on the other team's side of the field.

Freeze situations, encourage the players, and give praise for a successful leave. Also, try to play with even-numbered teams.

Point System:

- 1 point for a successful leave or a regular goal.
- 2 points for a successful leave and a shot on goal.
- 3 points for a successful leave and a goal.

11⚽

Overlapping

The marking techniques used in modern soccer are so effective that new methods of attacking plays are constantly emerging. One method is *overlapping*. With overlapping, a ball handler gets help from a teammate who rushes up at the sides and takes over the ball and creates new passing possibilities in the depth of the field. Usually overlapping is used to pass the opponents on the sidelines. We show two examples in Figures 11.1 and 11.2.

In Figure 11.1 the attacking right wing (RW) is driving the ball toward the defending left back (LB), challenging him or her. The attacking right midfielder (RMF) is running up the line, passing by both players. When the RMF starts the rush, shout a command, "keep the ball," to let the RW know that he or she is on the way. While the rusher is passing, the LB has a dilemma. He or she does not know if the ball handler will

- pass forward to the onrushing teammate,
- fake the pass and turn toward the goal, or
- make a pass toward the midfield.

In overlapping, the pass should come whenever the rusher passes the ball handler. It cannot be a side pass because that is difficult to control when a player is running fast. The ball must be played in depth so that the rusher can continue at a very fast speed.

Right and left wings are also called outside right and left forwards. Right and left halfbacks are also called outside or inside right and left midfielders. Right and left fullbacks are called right and left outside or inside fullbacks.

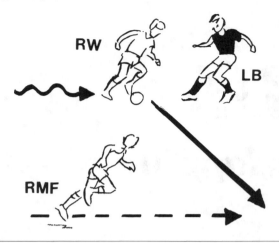

Figure 11.1 Standard overlapping procedure.

It is also important that the rusher does not run too close to the ball handler but keeps a good passing distance. Doing it this way will help the ball handler if he or she chooses to pass the ball to the onrushing player in Figure 11.1.

The situation in Figure 11.2 is similar to the one in Figure 11.1. The only difference is that the ball handler (RW) gets help from a center forward (CF) who comes around instead of along the sidelines (as in Figure 11.1).

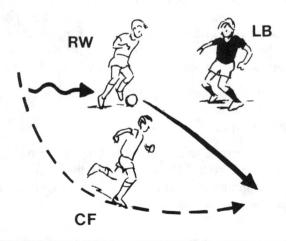

Figure 11.2 Overlapping variation.

Overlapping requires a lot from the players. You should wait to teach this section until the players learn to execute the pass well. They should also have had a chance to practice feinting before you introduce overlapping. Don't force the idea and don't expect results too fast. Give the players time to practice the different moves.

Exercise 1	Overlapping for seven- to nine-year-olds

Two Against One Plus One Goalie

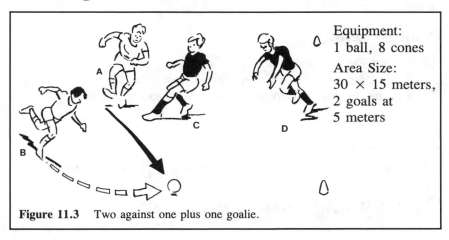

Equipment:
1 ball, 8 cones

Area Size:
30 × 15 meters,
2 goals at
5 meters

Figure 11.3   Two against one plus one goalie.

Organization

A and B attack C with D as goalie. A drives the ball challenging C. Depending on how C reacts, A plays a ball in depth to B who either charges with the ball or dribbles past C. The attack is finished with a shot on D. After a goal, save, or miss, or when C breaks up the play and passes back to goalie D, the attack is finished. C and D then attack A with B as goalie.

Note. The defenders change position every other attack.

Instructions

Instruct the defending players to meet the ball handler in midfield, being passive in the beginning so that the pass can be executed in depth to the overlapping player.

Soon the defender will become more active. The ball handler must then decide if he or she should pass or use a pass feint and dribble past the defender. Stress the following instruction points at the overlap:

- The ball handler must challenge the opposition.
- Teammates should call "keep the ball" and rush on the outside, passing the ball handler.
- When the teammate passes by, the ball handler has two options:

    Pass in depth to the teammate.

    Fake a pass to the teammate but drive the ball to the other side (inside) of the defender.

Direct the play so that the players will try to use overlaps or pass feints as much as possible.

Point System:

- 1 point for a regular goal.
- 1 point for a successful overlap and a pass feint.
- 3 points for an overlap plus a goal or a pass feint plus a goal.

Exercise 2	Overlapping for seven- to nine-year-olds

Overlapping: Assist or Shoot

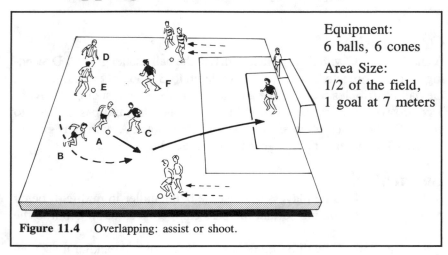

Equipment:
6 balls, 6 cones

Area Size:
1/2 of the field,
1 goal at 7 meters

Figure 11.4 Overlapping: assist or shoot.

Organization

A drives the ball toward C (five to ten meters outside the penalty area) and challenges C. B runs on the outside. A can pass to B or dribble toward the middle of the field. If A dribbles, he or she must complete the attack and take a shot on goal. If B gets the ball, he or she must drive toward the touch line and pass to A in front of the goal. C tries at all times to stop A from scoring. Then D and E go against F. The two goalies change after four attacks.

Instructions

The ball handler must challenge the defender. The pass must be made in depth so that the overlapping player doesn't have to stop to control the ball.

Exercise 1	Overlapping for ten- to fourteen-year-olds

Two Against One Plus One Goalie (Three Team Principle)

Equipment:
1–3 balls, 8 cones

Area Size:
40 × 20 meters,
2 goals at 5 meters

Figure 11.5   Two against one plus one goalie.

Organization

A and B attack C with D as goalie. A drives the ball and challenges C. When B overlaps, A observes and keeps the ball. Depending on C's reactions, A gives a pass in the depth for B to either rush with or dribble past C. The players try to finish with a shot on D. Then C and D take a ball at the right side of the goal and attack E with F as goalie. At that time,

A and B pick up their own ball and wait at the right side goal. When C and D finish the attack, E and F take their ball to the left side goal and attack A with B goalie.

Instructions
Encourage the defenders to meet the attackers at midfield. Instruct the defenders on points of overlapping. (See the instructions to this chapter and Overlapping for seven- to nine-year-olds, Exercise 1.)

Point System:

- 1 point for a regular goal.
- 1 point for overlapping and a pass feint.
- 3 points for overlapping plus a goal, or a pass feint plus a goal.

Exercise 2	Overlapping for ten- to fourteen-year-olds

Four Against Two Plus Two Goalies

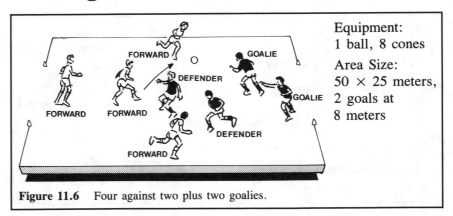

Equipment:
1 ball, 8 cones

Area Size:
50 × 25 meters,
2 goals at
8 meters

Figure 11.6   Four against two plus two goalies.

Organization
The white-shirt team (with four forwards) attacks the black-shirt team (two defenders and two goalies). The white-shirt team tries to get into scoring position. Whenever the white-shirt team misses the attack, the black-shirt team starts an attack with four forwards against the defenders and two goalies.

Instructions

Instruct the defenders not to back up too far toward their own goal. The attackers should try to create a two-on-one situation and then get around on the outside.

Direct the play toward more overlapping.

Point System:

- 1 point for a regular goal.
- 1 point for overlapping.
- 3 points for overlapping and a goal.

Exercise 3	Overlapping for ten- to fourteen-year-olds

Five Against Three Plus One Goalie

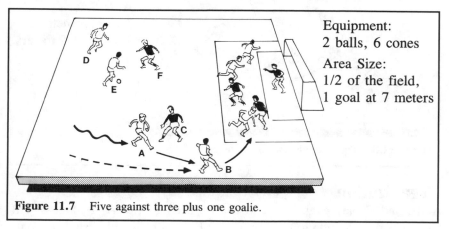

Equipment:
2 balls, 6 cones

Area Size:
1/2 of the field,
1 goal at 7 meters

Figure 11.7   Five against three plus one goalie.

Organization

The white-shirt team starts an attack by A and B using a two-on-one situation to get past C. B attacks on the outside. A can then play a ball in the depth so that B can rush for it, or A can dribble past C. In both cases the attack is executed as in a game. C plays defense as in a game. The white-shirt team has three forwards and the black-shirt team has two field players and one goalie who can only play inside the penalty area. The next attack is started with D and E trying to use a two-on-one situation to get past F.

Instructions

The players should use overlapping to get by the opposition. The ball handler should challenge the opposition. If he or she moves toward the middle, he or she creates larger open areas for the overlapping player. This player should run at high speed whenever passing by the defender. The passes must be played in the depth. The passes should be executed so that the overlapper can make a setup pass with the first touch of the ball.

Exercise 4	Overlapping for ten- to fourteen-year-olds

Three Against Two Plus One Goalie

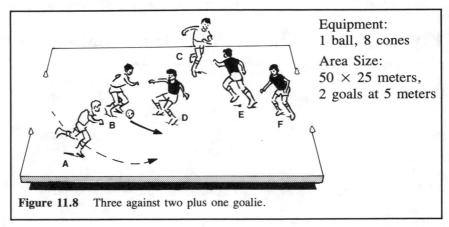

Equipment:
1 ball, 8 cones

Area Size:
50 × 25 meters,
2 goals at 5 meters

Figure 11.8   Three against two plus one goalie.

Organization

A, B, and C play against D and E with F as goalie. A, B, and C will try to use overlapping to get past D and E and finish with a shot on goal. After a finished attack, D, E, and F start an attack against A and B with C as goalie.

Instructions

The attacking team must look for opportunities to use overlapping to get past the opposition. Stress that the ball handler must challenge the opposition. You can direct the play toward more overlapping by counting a successful overlap as a goal.

Let the players use passing feints as alternatives to overlapping. After executing the play, the ball handler passes by the defender.

Because the attackers have opposing players it is more difficult to create successful overlapping.

Point System:

- 1 point for a normal goal.
- 1 point for overlapping or a passing feint.
- 3 points for overlapping and a goal, or a passing feint and a goal.

| Exercise 5 | Overlapping for ten- to fourteen-year-olds |

Four Against Three Plus One Goalie (Three Team Principle)

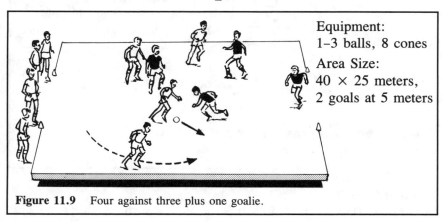

Equipment:
1–3 balls, 8 cones

Area Size:
40 × 25 meters,
2 goals at 5 meters

Figure 11.9   Four against three plus one goalie.

Organization

The white-shirt team attacks with four forwards. The black-shirt team has three defenders and a goalie. The attacking players should try to create two-on-one situations and, with the help of overlapping play, get by the opposition.

After a successful attack, the black-shirt team with four forwards attacks the striped-shirt team that has three defenders and a goalie. Next, the striped-shirt team attacks the white-shirt team.

Instructions

The players in the attacking team should always be alert to situations in which they can use overlapping and pass a defender on the outside.

Point System:

- 1 point for a regular goal.
- 1 point for overlapping.
- 3 points for overlapping and a goal.

Exercise 6	Overlapping for ten- to fourteen-year-olds

Six Against Five Plus One Goalie

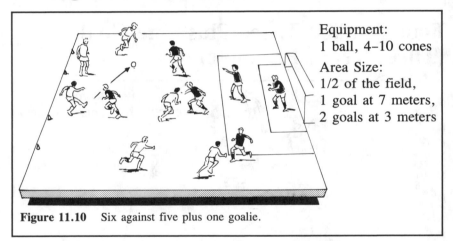

Equipment:
1 ball, 4–10 cones

Area Size:
1/2 of the field,
1 goal at 7 meters,
2 goals at 3 meters

Figure 11.10   Six against five plus one goalie.

Organization
The white-shirt team has six forwards and attacks the black-shirt team with five forwards and a goalie.

The white-shirt players try to create a two-on-one situation on the sidelines and use these for overlapping. The players on the black-shirt team try to score in one of the small goals.

Instructions
At this point, many of your players may have become specialists in their team positions. If that is the case, let them play their regular positions.

Instruct the players on the white-shirt team to look for situations that are suitable for overlapping. (See this chapter's introduction and Overlapping for seven- to nine-year-olds, Exercise 1.)

Whenever the overlapping players reach the ball, they should, as quickly as possible and preferably with one-touch, make a lay-up. These are most effective when they are hard and directed at the area outside of the front post. Also, a pass to the outside of the rear post is difficult for the goalie to reach.

Point System:

- 1 point for a goal.
- 1 point for overlapping.
- 3 points for a goal after overlapping.

12 ⚽

Defensive Plays

When the basics of attacking plays are fully understood, you can begin to practice defensive plays. In the ten-year-old group, or perhaps later depending on how advanced the players are, it is proper to start teaching the basics of defensive plays.

When the opposing team has the ball the entire team should be defending. It is important that the players regroup from an attacking to a defensive posture whenever the opposition gets the ball. Defense builds on organization and discipline. This means that players on a team losing the ball are able to regroup to a defensive posture toward the opposing player. To be on the defense means that one is closer to his or her own goal than the opposing player is.

Marking

Marking means that a player is on a line between the opposing player and his or her own goal. The marking player should be in a position to allow sight of both the opposing player and the ball (see Figure 12.1).

Zone marking means to divide the field in three zones lengthwise. Every player is responsible for a zone and should mark every player appearing in that zone. Zone areas will vary depending on the opposition's positions. In this marking system the defenders change marking assignments as marked players move from zone to zone.

Figure 12.1 Proper marking positions.

One-on-one marking implies that the defending player marks an opposing player regardless of where the player is positioned on the field. When your own team has the ball, the defenders should participate in the attack.

Point marking is the most extreme form of one-on-one marking. The defending player is totally committed to the defense and does not participate in the attack. This method should be used only when the opposing team has an especially good player.

Combination marking should be used as a standard. It implies a combination of zone and one-on-one markings. Within respective zones, the defenders mark players who are in the zone. If, during an attack, the players change zones, the defenders will follow as in one-on-one marking. However, if a player changes zones in a slow situation or when the play is dead, the defender stays in the correct zone and marks any player who comes into that zone.

Press

The ball handler is immediately attacked by the closest defender to slow down or prevent a good kick, pass, or dribble execution (Figure 12.2). The advantage of the press is that it creates regrouping time for support and coverage by the defensive players.

Figure 12.2 The press.

Support and Coverage

Defensive plays require depth. The defenders should never be lined up across the field. One good cross or through pass can penetrate the entire line. To play and create proper depth, one must distinguish between support and coverage.

One gives support to a teammate who is pressing or challenged by a ball handler. If the teammate is overplayed, the supporting player must take over (see Figure 12.3).

The farther away from the ball a player is, the looser he or she can be with point marking. Instead, cover *play areas* behind teammates.

Many teams are presently giving assignments to a player who has no marking responsibilities. Instead, he or she devotes all efforts to support and coverage. This player, often called *libero* or *sweeper*, should try to move in line with the ball and the goal and should be closer to the goal than the marked player (Figure 12.4).

Thanks to the setup with a sweeper, the defending team will usually have more players defending than the attacking team has attacking on the

Figure 12.3 Providing support.

Figure 12.4 The libero provides support and coverage.

defending half of the field. Therefore, the defenders are numerically superior.

In attack plays, one of the inside defenders should support the attack. Often this player has an advantage, coming from an open, unmarked position.

If the attacking team, too optimistically, lets the sweeper and inside defenders go too far up in the attack, a dangerous situation is created when they lose the ball. These players do not have enough time to get back to the defense and suddenly the defenders are numerically shorthanded.

When this happens, it becomes the duty of the defender closest to the ball to try to delay the attacker, gaining time for the defense to hustle back and regroup.

Exercise 1	Defense for ten- to fourteen-year-olds

Two Against One Plus One Goalie

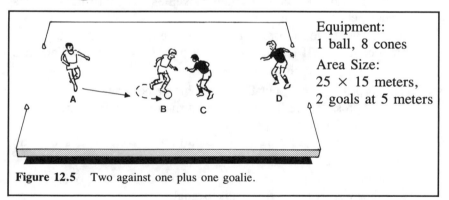

Equipment:
1 ball, 8 cones

Area Size:
25 × 15 meters,
2 goals at 5 meters

Figure 12.5   Two against one plus one goalie.

Organization

A and B attack C with D as goalie. After an attack, goal, goal save, or shot outside, or if C takes away the ball and passes to the goalie, C and D start an attack against B with A as goalie.

The practice is based on B and C's playing one-on-one. The other players, A and D, are only there to give support and should never be in front of the other team players or finish the attacks. All players change tasks after each attack.

Instructions

Stress the following points for the defenders in one-on-one situations:

1. If A gives support to the ball handler, C should be
   - on the defending side of B,
   - on the imaginary line between attacker and own goal (goal side),
   - as close to the opposition as possible to break up the play before the opposition gets the ball (marking), and
   - in such a position that he or she sees both the ball and the opposition.

2. Whenever A passes to B, C should mark closely so that he or she can break up the pass and get the ball if
   - A or B makes some mistake in their efforts,
   - A makes a bad pass (e.g., too sloppy, too hard, wrong direction),
   - B has bad control while receiving, or
   - the coordination between their movements is poor (the pass does not get to B in rhythm).

   Do not mark too closely or A can make a pass in the dangerous area behind C. If B reaches the ball first, C is overplayed and has a free path to goal.

3. If A's pass reaches, but B still has his or her back to the goal, C should press so closely that B can't turn around with the ball. Then B's only chance is to play back to A.

4. If B succeeds in turning with the ball under control, C should do the following:
   - Wait if he or she has no support and should not be overplayed, otherwise B has a free path to goal.
   - Force B into a specific direction. C should force B toward the sidelines. C is placed in such a way that the path to the middle of the field is covered.
   - Try to give B as bad a position as possible for the finishing attack.

a	b

Figure 12.6 Turning 180° (a) and turning 90° (b).

It is important that you show the defenders how to position their feet so that a turn can be made quickly to catch the attacker dribbling by.

The defender should make a 90-degree rather than a 180-degree turn. A player turning 180 degrees is approximately one meter slower in the first five meters than a player turning 90 degrees (Figure 12.6).

Test the players so they get to know the difference. Have two players sprint five meters. One must start with the back toward the running direction. It is necessary for this player to turn 180 degrees. The other player can start keeping feet parallel with the starting line, 90 degrees to the running direction. For that player, it is necessary only to turn 90 degrees before starting to run.

The player who turns only 90 degrees will win by one meter on a five-meter sprint. The player turning 180 degrees can also lose balance very easily.

More assurance can be achieved if the players change tasks. The second 90-degree player wins with approximately the same margin.

| Exercise 2 | Defense for ten- to fourteen-year-olds |

Three Against Two Plus One Goalie

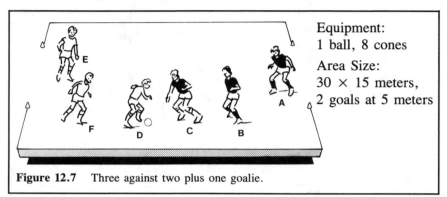

Equipment:
1 ball, 8 cones

Area Size:
30 × 15 meters,
2 goals at 5 meters

Figure 12.7   Three against two plus one goalie.

Organization

D will try to score after dribbling past two defenders, B and C. D has two teammates, E and F, who can give support only and cannot pass by D or finish an attack. Of the defenders, C will be a true defender against D, and B will cover and give support.

When the attack is finished the other team starts an attack. All attacks start at a team's own goal line; there should be no long passes. A, who is supported by B and C, should dribble past E and F, with D as goalie. In this exercise you can also use your team goalie whenever his or her team is defending.

Instructions

Numerical advantage should now be given to the defenders. The chances to break up the attack are, therefore, good. In this exercise B and C defend one attacker, D, depending on how the exercise is directed.

Demonstrate with your team's best dribbler as D before all others start the drill. Stress the following instructional points for defenders in numerical advantage where the following situations can occur for the defenders, B and C.

1. When E or F are ball handlers, then C marks D; and B covers.
2. When E or F plays a pass to D, the same rules govern for C as in 1; B covers.

3. If D has received a pass from E or F with the back to the attacking direction, C presses D to obstruct a turn with the ball; and B covers.
4. If D successfully turns in the attacking direction, then, C presses D; and B gives support to C.

A good supporting position means that the player is on the imaginary line between the ball and goal, and at approximately a five-meter distance. Then a supporting player can best attack an opposing player who dribbles past a teammate. Young players must realize how important it is to get close enough when giving support.

If the ball handler, after overplaying the pressing defender, gets a one-on-one situation against the person supporting, the distance is too far.

When advancing, the supporter will adjust his or her position to the pressing player. If he or she tries to force the attacker in a specific direction (e.g., toward the sidelines), the supporter can count on the challenger trying to force the play to the sideline. The starting position will be better if the supporter can move closer to the sidelines to get the ball or to start pressing if the teammate is overtaken.

It is very important that the players talk with each other and gain good understanding of each other in these situations. How to coach talking in the game can be found in chapter 5.

| Exercise 3 | Defense for ten- to fourteen-year-olds |

Six Against Two (The Square)

Equipment:
1 ball, 4 cones

Area Size:
10 × 10 meters

Figure 12.8   Six against two.

Organization

Play with six players against two in the middle. These two try playing together to break up the plays. This is done through pressing and coverage. After the two in the middle break up the play three times, they change with two other players. The play is broken up when a defender touches the ball.

Instructions

In this exercise, pressing is practiced. Aggressiveness against the ball handler pays off.

The defenders' judgment is important in determining when they should try to touch the ball and break up the play.

The player who does not press gives no support, as in Exercises 1 and 2, because no ball handler intends to dribble past the pressing player. Instead, the player should cover the play areas where passes could go.

The pressing player can now, in his or her own way, force the ball handler to direct the pass in one predetermined direction.

The cooperation between the two defenders is coached in the square. Switching between press coverage happens fast for the two. A pass can change the situation very quickly, and the tasks change instantly.

See Passing for ten- to fourteen-year-olds, Exercise 1, regarding attacking plays in the square.

Exercise 4	Defense for ten- to fourteen-year-olds

Two Against Two Plus Two Goalies

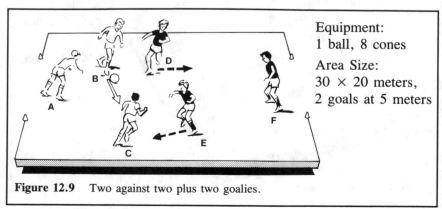

Equipment:
1 ball, 8 cones

Area Size:
30 × 20 meters,
2 goals at 5 meters

Figure 12.9   Two against two plus two goalies.

Organization

B and C play against D and E. The goalie on the attacking team can be used for back passes. After finished attacks you can change goalies so that E and F with D as goalie attack A and B with C as goalie. You can also play with a regular goalie setup.

Instructions

In small team plays with the same number of players on each team, the defenders often serve a relieving function by changing positions.

No exact task distribution can be realized among the players because the tasks change. If B is the ball handler, D should challenge and E should give support. If B passes to C there is a new situation. E changes to pressing C while D is giving support.

Exercise 5   Defense for ten- to fourteen-year-olds

Three Against Three Plus Two Goalies

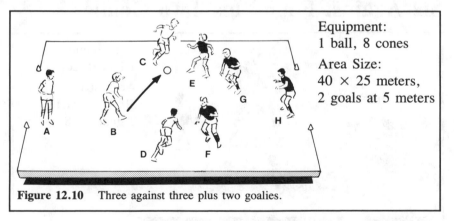

Equipment:
1 ball, 8 cones

Area Size:
40 × 25 meters,
2 goals at 5 meters

Figure 12.10   Three against three plus two goalies.

Organization

Play with a libero (sweeper). B is libero on the attacking team, and G is libero on the defending team. The game is directed so that the libero on the attacking team may not pass midfield.

Play for periods of three minutes and change tasks within the team. Goalies do not change roles.

Instructions

In this exercise the defending team is playing with numerical advantage on their own side of the field. The team can then create a definite task distribution. Two of the midfield players, E and F, are marking the opposing players. The libero should not have a marking responsibility; rather that player concentrates only on support and coverage.

The advantage with predetermined assignments is that all players know exactly what to do. This provides room for fewer mistakes. The libero should always support the player pressing the opposition if that player is turned in the attacking direction. Thereby, a two-on-one situation is created to the defenders' advantage.

Whenever libero B is the ball handler, G should be placed so that he or she can quickly give support to both teammates to cooperate in the same manner as in Exercises 1 and 2.

Exercise 6	Defense for ten- to fourteen-year-olds

Six Against Four Plus Two Goalies

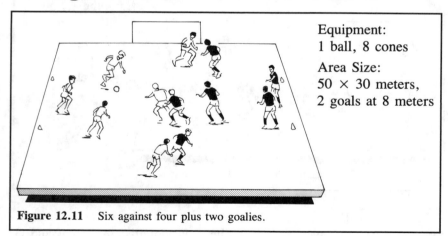

Equipment:
1 ball, 8 cones

Area Size:
50 × 30 meters,
2 goals at 8 meters

Figure 12.11   Six against four plus two goalies.

Organization

Play with six players on each team. The attacking team should always have three players on the forward line, two players in midfield who cannot go past the midfield line or finish an attack, and a play maker in the back field. The defending team plays with three marking fullbacks, one libero, and two goalies. After ten attacks the players change tasks.

Instructions

Three different tactics can be practiced in this exercise: zone, one-on-one, and combination. On their own side of the field, the defenders have a numerical advantage, four against three. Instructions in defensive plays from Exercises 2 and 5 can also be used.

What happens if the ball handler in the attacking team passes to the forward on the right wing (all seen from a defender's point of view)? In Figure 12.12a the midfielder is the ball handler. In Figure 12.12b, the defender adjusts after a pass when the ball handler is allowed to turn to the attacking direction.

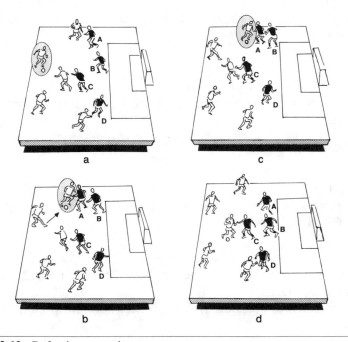

a

c

b

d

Figure 12.12 Defensive strategies.

Player A

- presses the ball handler, and
- forces the opposition against the sideline.

Player B

- gives support to A,
- directs A, and
- is prepared to press if the ball handler passes by A.

Player C

- marks the midfield attackers, and
- is prepared to press if his or her opposing player becomes ball handler.

Player D

- covers areas to the left and behind C, and
- is prepared to press the left wing if he or she becomes ball handler.

What happens if the ball handler in Figure 12.12b passes forward to the midfield? The positions before and after the pass are shown in Figures 12.12c and d.

Player C

- presses the ball handler, and
- forces the opposing player in a predetermined direction, in this case to the right.

Player B

- gives support to C,
- directs C, and
- is prepared to press the ball handler if he or she passes C—probably on C's right side.

Players A and D

- cover the areas on the right side and on the left side of B and, if needed, behind B; and,
- are prepared to press the right or the left forward if either of them gets a pass.

Exercise 7	Defense for ten- to fourteen-year-olds

Five Against Five With Two Goalies

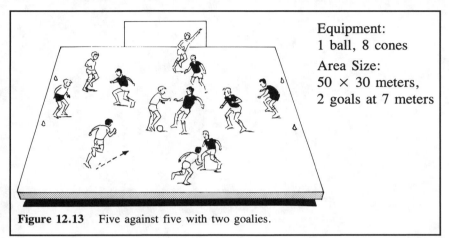

Equipment:
1 ball, 8 cones

Area Size:
50 × 30 meters,
2 goals at 7 meters

Figure 12.13   Five against five with two goalies.

Organization
Each team plays with five field players and a goalie.

Instructions
The purpose of this drill is to teach the players how to regroup from attacking to defensive play. In the defense it is important to follow what is learned in Exercises 1 through 6.

13⚽

Shooting

It is the number of successful shots on goal that determines the outcome of a match. Therefore, you should, as often as possible, finish your practice session with shots on goal. To get a concentrated and more effective shooting practice, you should take it out of the regular practice and treat it as a special session.

Do plenty of shooting practice, especially during the outdoor season. Shooting practice should be combined with goalie practice. Allow all the players in the seven- to nine-year-old group to practice both regular as well as goalie plays.

Go through the preliminary practice as quickly as possible. In most situations during the game a shooter is usually under some pressure. Therefore, the same conditions should prevail in practice.

<table>
<tr><td>Exercise 1</td><td>Shooting for seven- to nine-year-olds</td></tr>
</table>

Shot Against Goalie

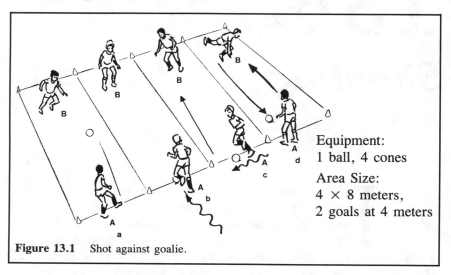

Equipment:
1 ball, 4 cones
Area Size:
4 × 8 meters,
2 goals at 4 meters

Figure 13.1 Shot against goalie.

Organization
Refer to Figure 13.1:

(a) A places the ball on the goal line, takes a shot on a stationary ball, and tries to score on B. Record who makes the most goals on ten shots.

(b) A starts approximately five meters behind the line, dribbles the ball forward, and takes a shot at the line. Then B does the same, and so on.

(c) A drives the ball a few meters along the line and shoots at B. Then B does the same.

(d) B rolls the ball to A who meets it on his or her side of the line and takes a direct shot. Then A rolls the ball to B who takes a direct shot.

Instructions
Let all players practice one alternative (a–d). It is better to have ample time to practice one type of shot than to rush and try to do too many.

Occasionally change the exercise so that players have to shoot with the "wrong foot": left foot for right-footers and vice versa.

Exercise 2

Shooting for seven- to nine-year-olds

Pass-Shoot

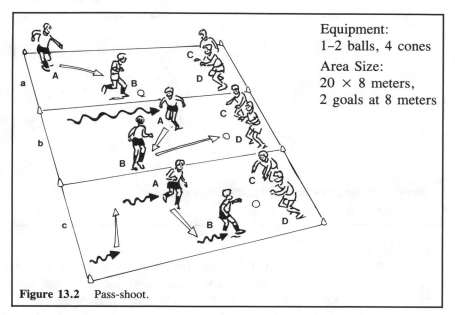

Equipment:
1–2 balls, 4 cones

Area Size:
20 × 8 meters,
2 goals at 8 meters

Figure 13.2 Pass-shoot.

Organization
Refer to Figure 13.2:

(a) A plays a pass toward midfield. B rushes up and takes a direct shot off the pass. C and D are goalies. Then C passes to D, who shoots on A and B. Record which team scores the highest on ten tries.

(b) A drives the ball a few meters past midfield and passes backward in an angle to B, who takes a shot. C and D are goalies. Then C drives the ball and passes backward to D who shoots on A and B.

(c) A and B pass to each other, driving the ball forward toward midfield where one of them takes a shot. C and D are goalies. Then C and D pass to each other, driving the ball forward toward midfield where one of them takes a shot.

Instructions
The players should always take turns shooting. Make sure they take shots off passes both from the left and from the right.

Exercise 3   Shooting for seven- to nine-year-olds

One-on-One Plus Goalie

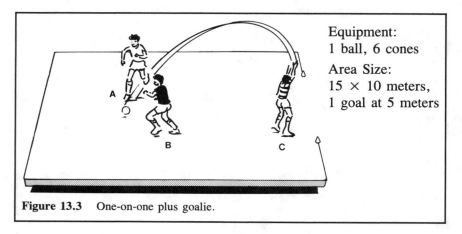

Equipment:
1 ball, 6 cones

Area Size:
15 × 10 meters,
1 goal at 5 meters

Figure 13.3 One-on-one plus goalie.

Organization

Goalie C, facing the goal, throws the ball backward overhead. A and B try to get to the ball, competing to see who can score the most goals. A larger goal size encourages shots on goal. Limit the time, and change tasks.

Instructions

You can also let A or B start the attack fifteen meters from the goal. This means that he or she should fake and take a shot as quickly as possible. The body feint is a good way to create space for a shot with one-on-one. Instruct the feint. (See Feints for seven- to nine-year-olds, Exercise 5.)

Stress that the exercise is a shooting drill; the feint is secondary. Everyone should try to get into a shooting position as quickly as possible.

Exercise 4

Shooting for seven- to nine-year-olds

Two Against One Plus One Goalie

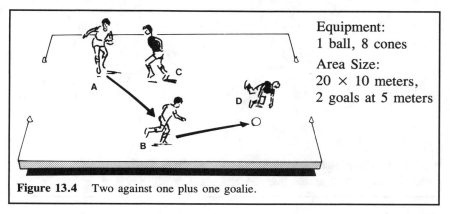

Equipment:
1 ball, 8 cones

Area Size:
20 × 10 meters,
2 goals at 5 meters

Figure 13.4 Two against one plus one goalie.

Organization

A and B attack C with D as goalie. A and B should try to get into shooting position as quickly as possible. Direct the exercise so that A and B attack ten times. Thereafter, change tasks between the teams.

Instructions

The ball handler has two options. He or she can pass to the teammate and quickly get to a new position, or he or she can fake a pass and dribble past the opposition. Repeat the passing feint. The teammate of the ball handler should avoid the passing shadow.

The play distance cannot be too short or the pass receiver has too little time to control the ball and cannot shoot before the defense covers the shot.

Three Against Two Plus One Goalie

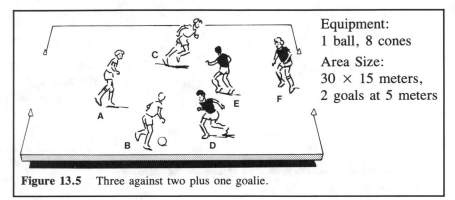

Equipment:
1 ball, 8 cones

Area Size:
30 × 15 meters,
2 goals at 5 meters

Figure 13.5   Three against two plus one goalie.

Organization

A, B, and C attack D and E with F as goalie. A, B, or C will try to get into shooting position and take a shot as quickly as possible. Let the teams change tasks after ten attacks.

Instructions

Make sure that the players try to get into shooting position as quickly as possible. One way to direct this drill is to score 2 points for every goal that is a result of less than four passes.

If the players get too close to the goal before they shoot, place markers (cones) approximately seven meters from the goal line, marking the closest point from which a shot can be taken. Let players score from a closer point with the "wrong" foot.

Exercise 1   Shooting for ten- to fourteen-year-olds

Shooting Competition

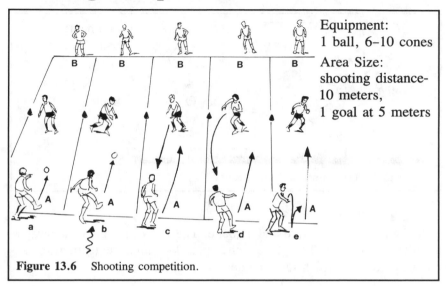

Equipment:
1 ball, 6–10 cones

Area Size:
shooting distance–
10 meters,
1 goal at 5 meters

Figure 13.6   Shooting competition.

Organization
Refer to Figure 13.6:

(a) A and B alternately shoot a stationary ball. See who can score the most on ten shots.

(b) A dribbles the ball approximately five meters and shoots. Then B dribbles and shoots.

(c) The goalie rolls the ball to A who meets it (not over the line) and takes a direct shot. Then B takes a shot on a rolling ball.

(d) The goalie tosses the ball in an arc to A who collects the ball and shoots. Then B collects the ball and shoots.

(e) A drops the ball in front, lets it bounce, and shoots a volley or half volley. Then B does the same.

Instructions
In this drill you put many players in goal. They cannot touch the ball with the hands. Make the goals four meters wide, and count only goals below waistline height.

Move as quickly as possible from this exercise to shooting practice in small team games.

Exercise 2

One-on-One With Two Goalies

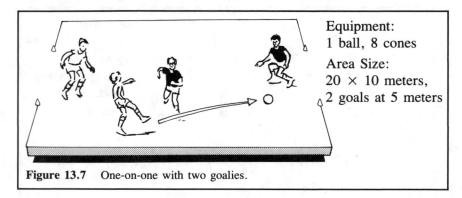

Equipment:
1 ball, 8 cones

Area Size:
20 × 10 meters,
2 goals at 5 meters

Figure 13.7   One-on-one with two goalies.

Organization
Both teams have a forward and a goalie. The size of the goal encourages the players to shoot. The players change tasks within the team after two minutes. Record which team attains the highest score.

Instructions
Occasionally direct the exercise toward shots with the wrong foot by scoring double for these goals.

Exercise 3   Shooting for ten- to fourteen-year-olds

NASL Penalty Kick

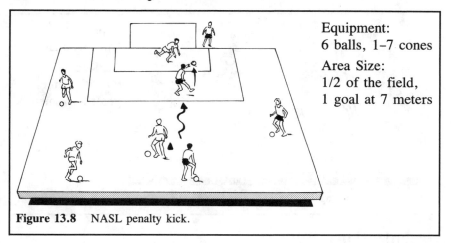

Equipment:
6 balls, 1–7 cones

Area Size:
1/2 of the field,
1 goal at 7 meters

Figure 13.8 NASL penalty kick.

Organization

Tie games in the NASL (North American Soccer League) were finished in the following manner. A player starts with the ball thirty meters from the goal. At the same time, the goalie comes out to meet the player. The ball handler must take a shot on goal within five seconds, otherwise the attack is over. After that, the other team repeats the same procedures.

Have two four-person teams of three penalty takers and a goalie compete.

Instructions

The attacking player is met by an onrushing goalie and has to work under time pressure. He or she must decide quickly on the best way to score.

Exercise 4   Shooting for ten- to fourteen-year-olds

Four Against Three Plus One Goalie

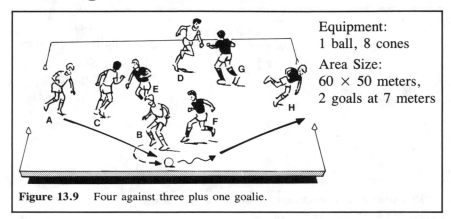

Equipment:
1 ball, 8 cones

Area Size:
60 × 50 meters,
2 goals at 7 meters

Figure 13.9   Four against three plus one goalie.

Organization
The white-shirt team (four players) attacks the black-shirt team (three players and one goalie). After a finished attack, the teams change tasks.

Instructions
You can encourage fast finishes of the attacks by counting double points for goals that are scored after less than five passes between the attacking team members.

Exercise 5   Shooting for ten- to fourteen-year-olds

Three Against Three With One Extra Against One Goal

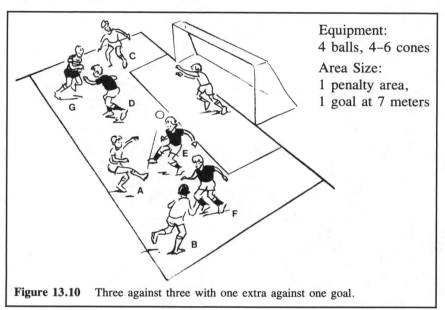

Equipment:
4 balls, 4–6 cones

Area Size:
1 penalty area,
1 goal at 7 meters

Figure 13.10   Three against three with one extra against one goal.

Organization
A, B, and C play against D, E, and F within the penalty area. Player G, who is the reserve, is always on the team that gets the ball after the goalie throws it out, backward, and over the head. A team attacks until it has taken a shot on goal or until the defending team breaks up the play and plays back to the goalie. If the ball is played outside the penalty area, the attacking team will get it back and continue the attack.

Instructions
You can let the teams start every other attack from the penalty box line directly in front of the goal. The reserve player always belongs to the team that is attacking.

14 ⚽

Heading

Soccer should be played as much as possible on the ground so that it is easier for the pass receiver to control the ball and continue the play. Often, the ball is in the air, especially at goal kicks, throw-ins, and corner kicks. Good heading technique in front of the goal becomes most important to the final game result. In these situations an offensive player must be able to score with a header or pass with the head to another player in open scoring position. A defensive player should be able to head out the high balls from a dangerous zone.

Learning good head plays should begin at an early age and as early in the season as possible. You must teach the art correctly to avoid the fear most players have in the beginning.

It is important to practice with light and dry balls. Many players have a fear of heading balls, remembering some past experience with heavy and hard balls or the use of wrong techniques.

Heading is as important for young players as it is for the pros, and it should be worked on from the beginning and constantly repeated and improved.

Exercise 1   Heading for seven- to nine-year-olds

Head Against Goal After Toss

Equipment:
1 ball, 4 cones

Area Size:
4 × 4 meters,
2 goals at
4 meters

Figure 14.1 Head against goal after toss.

Organization
A tosses the ball straight up and heads. B is goalie and tries to save the goal. Then B heads against A who acts as goalie. Record which player has the higher score in ten tries.

Instructions
Rotate the players and give proper heading instructions, using the following points of instruction (see figure 14.2):

- Head the ball with the forehead.
- Look at the ball—don't close the eyes.
- Bend your body backward above the waist, then quickly forward to make a powerful header.

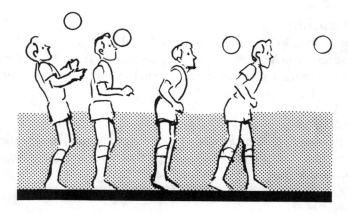

Figure 14.2 Proper heading techniques.

| Exercise 2 | Heading for seven- to nine-year-olds |

Head Against Goal on Pass From Front

Equipment:
1 ball, 4 cones

Area Size:
4 × 4 meters,
2 goals at 4 meters

Figure 14.3 Head against goal on pass from front.

Organization

A throws the ball to B, who heads against goal. Change after ten headers.

The exercise can be intensified by higher throws from the goalie so that the other player must jump up to head the ball. Record which player scores the most goals.

Instructions

The jump should come early so that the player has time to flex the upper body, hang in the air (Figure 14.4), and get the upper body's forceful movement forward to give power to the header.

Figure 14.4 Hanging in the air.

Exercise 3   Heading for seven- to nine-year-olds

Head Against Goal on Pass From the Side

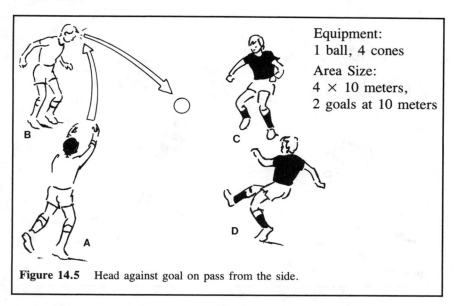

Equipment:
1 ball, 4 cones

Area Size:
4 × 10 meters,
2 goals at 10 meters

Figure 14.5   Head against goal on pass from the side.

Organization

Player A tosses the ball to B who heads against C and D who are acting as goalies. Then C tosses to D who heads against A and B's goal. The players take turns with tosses and headers. Increase the pace by having the heading players jump in the air before they head the ball. Record which team scores the most goals.

Instructions

- Head the ball with the forehead.
- Look at the ball—don't close the eyes.
- Bend your body backward above the waist, then quickly forward to make a powerful header.

| Exercise 4 | Heading for seven- to nine-year-olds |

Head Against Goal After Approach and Jump

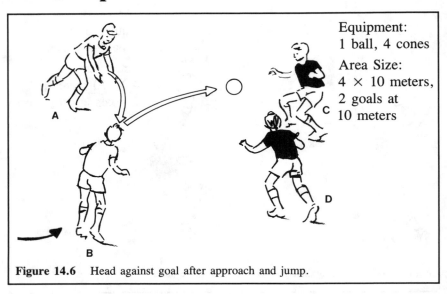

Equipment:
1 ball, 4 cones

Area Size:
4 × 10 meters,
2 goals at
10 meters

Figure 14.6   Head against goal after approach and jump.

Organization
A tosses the ball to B who, after an approach, jumps up and heads against goal. C tosses to D who approaches, jumps, and heads the ball, and so on. Record which team makes the most goals.

Instructions
The jump should come early so that the player has time to flex the upper body, hang in the air, and get the body's forceful movement forward to give power to the header.

Exercise 1   Heading for ten- to fourteen-year-olds

Throw–Head–Catch

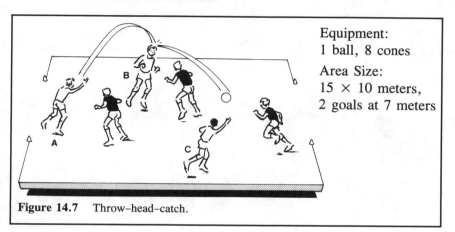

Equipment:
1 ball, 8 cones

Area Size:
15 × 10 meters,
2 goals at 7 meters

Figure 14.7   Throw–head–catch.

Organization

Play with three players on each team. A tosses to B. B heads to A or C who catches the ball and tosses to one of the teammates. The team tries to keep possession.

The opposing team can break up the plays with a header on a toss or with a catch after a header.

Whenever the ball touches the ground or goes outside the square, the team getting the ball first will start the game again.

Instructions

The players should freely move around the square either marking or making themselves open for a pass. No one can stand closer than one meter to the ball tosser. A goal can be scored only with a header.

You can also play with four players per team.

Exercise 2	Heading for ten- to fourteen-year-olds

Head Against Goal With Opposition

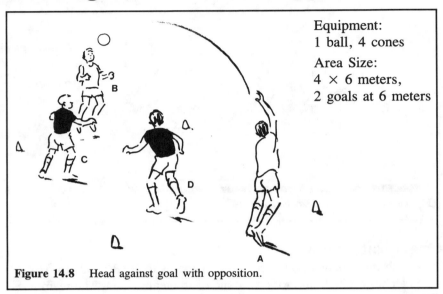

Equipment:
1 ball, 4 cones

Area Size:
4 × 6 meters,
2 goals at 6 meters

Figure 14.8   Head against goal with opposition.

Organization

A throws the ball over or to the side of C who is a passive defender. B jumps and heads the ball toward goal. D is goalie. After ten headers the other team takes over.

B cannot get in front of his or her own goal line when heading. Increase the pace slowly by letting C become more active in trying to head the ball. Record which team scores the most goals.

Instructions

Follow the previous guidelines for proper heading technique. The ball should be headed downward when attacking. Low balls to the post are more difficult for goalies to catch.

Heading for ten- to fourteen-year-olds

Head Against Goal on Pass From the Side With Opposition

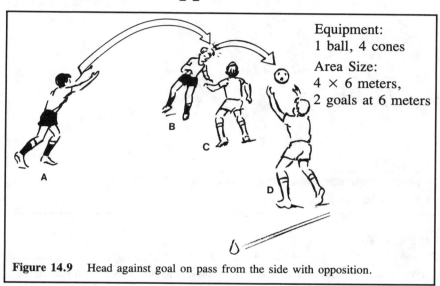

Equipment:
1 ball, 4 cones

Area Size:
4 × 6 meters,
2 goals at 6 meters

Figure 14.9 Head against goal on pass from the side with opposition.

Organization
D stands in goal. C marks B without hard pressure. A throws to B who approaches, jumps, and heads toward goal. B cannot go over his or her goal line to head. Record which team scores the highest on twenty headers.

Instructions
Follow the instructions for heading in Exercises 1 and 2 for seven- to nine-year-olds.

Exercise 4

Heading for ten- to fourteen-year-olds

Heading Game

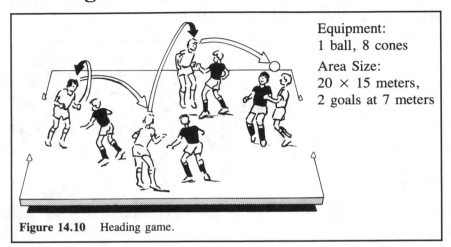

Equipment:
1 ball, 8 cones

Area Size:
20 × 15 meters,
2 goals at 7 meters

Figure 14.10 Heading game.

Organization

Play with four players on each team, and allow heading only. Start with a player tossing the ball to himself or herself and heading it to a teammate, who in turn heads to another player or back to the server. The opposition can break up the play at any time but only with a header. Whenever the ball goes outside the area or touches the ground, the team reaching the ball first will restart the play. To score the ball must be headed at least once. Goal kicks, corners, and throw-ins are started with a tossup and header. If someone touches the ball with the hands before it hits the ground, the other team gets a penalty header. You can develop these rules further.

Instructions

The players move freely all over the field, marking or trying to open up the play. Heading backward with a head sweep is not allowed. The risk of an accident is too great.

Exercise 5

Setup Header

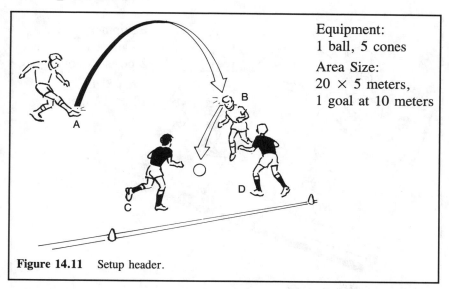

Equipment:
1 ball, 5 cones

Area Size:
20 × 5 meters,
1 goal at 10 meters

Figure 14.11   Setup header.

Organization

A sends the ball to B, who tries to head a goal against C and D. After ten headers A and B change. After ten more, the teams change tasks.

Instructions

This exercise requires that the players make a lay-up shot. The players should change the height of the lay-ups. For the low ball one may dive forward and head. Instruct to head downward.

Exercise 6

Heading for ten- to fourteen-year-olds

Header-Tennis

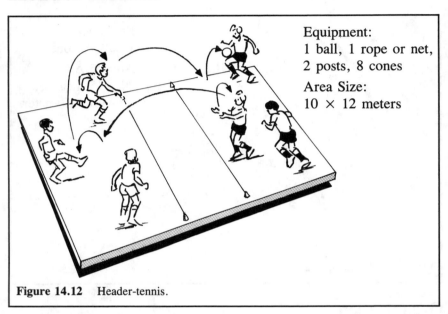

Equipment:
1 ball, 1 rope or net,
2 posts, 8 cones

Area Size:
10 × 12 meters

Figure 14.12 Header-tennis.

Organization

Play with three players on each team. One player tosses the ball to himself or herself and then heads it over the neutral area. The ball must touch the ground/floor after the serve to be in play. The ball can be played with feet, thighs, or head, but must be played over to the opposing side with the head. The teams can play the ball to each other before it's played over the net.

Instructions

Count points the same way as in volleyball or table tennis. Adjust the rules according to the players' abilities.

Exercise 7   Heading for ten- to fourteen-year-olds

Setup: Head Against Goal

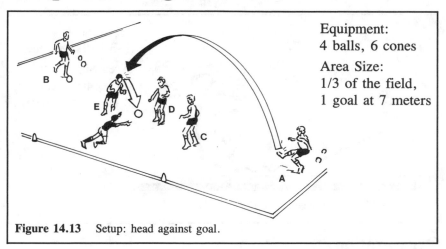

Equipment:
4 balls, 6 cones

Area Size:
1/3 of the field,
1 goal at 7 meters

Figure 14.13   Setup: head against goal.

Organization
The wings A and B take in turn a lay-up kick to their teammates C, D, and E, who try to head a goal. Increase the difficulty by putting in defenders. Change tasks after a preset number of lay-ups.

Instructions
Players A and B try to change the lay-ups, sometimes low and sometimes high. Players C, D, and E should try to place themselves correctly. They should not get too close to the goal before the pass is made. They should try to stay at the outside of the penalty area and charge the goal when the pass is made.

Exercise 8   Heading for ten- to fourteen-year-olds

Setup: Head Against Goal

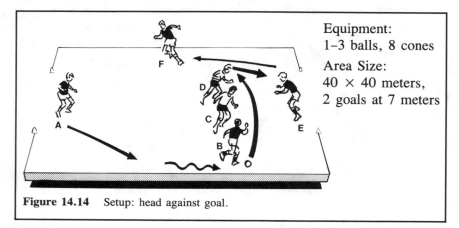

Equipment:
1–3 balls, 8 cones

Area Size:
40 × 40 meters,
2 goals at 7 meters

Figure 14.14   Setup: head against goal.

Organization

Play with two goalies, two wings, and two to four players heading. Goalie A throws the ball to wing B who meets it, turns, drives the ball, and lays it up to C or D who heads against the goal. Goalie E throws the ball to F who meets it, turns, drives the ball, and lays it up to E and D, who have turned around, and who now head the ball to goalie A, and so on. Change tasks after ten lay-ups.

Increase the pace by inserting two defenders against the heading players. The defenders should try to head the ball toward the wings. Record which team makes the most goals by heading.

Instructions

The lay-ups should be solid and should be directed toward the outside of the nearest post. The goalie has problems reaching this area. C and D should not be too close to the goal; rather they should be approximately fifteen meters from the goal to be able to judge from where the ball is coming before they rush forward to head. C and D should concentrate on the front post; E should concentrate on the rear or somewhere behind. If the ball comes too low the attack should be finished with a direct shot on goal.

Exercise 9

Heading for ten- to fourteen-year-olds

Small Team Play—Score Only on Header or Header Pass

Equipment:
1 ball, 8 cones

Area Size:
2 goals at 7 meters

Figure 14.15   Small team play.

Organization
Play with two small teams of six players each and no goalies. Goals can only be scored with a header or from a header pass.

Instructions
Instruct the players to keep good play width and attack on the sidelines to get good lay-up shots for headers or shots off headers.

15 ⚽

Goalie Practice

In the seven- to nine-year-old age group, practice is usually done in small groups or with small teams. Players should finish an attack with a shot on goal. Team goalies should have the chance to stop the shot. Most players should also have a chance to play goalie in practices of two-on-one plus one goalie.

The standard practice all players receive and goalie practice of the type just described are sufficient for seven- to nine-year-old players.

However, when players reach the ten- to fourteen-year-old age group, you should give special training during designated times to those who are interested.

There is always a player who shows more interest in the goalie task. This player should be given special goalie practice.

Figure 15.1 Two-goalie practice.

Figure 15.2 One player, two goalies.

Figure 15.3 Special goalie training is important after age ten.

Why Special Goalie Practice?

Goalies have greater responsibilities than any other player on the field. A forward's mistake can often be corrected by teammates. Goalie mistakes are decisive and can seldom be corrected.

One of the most important tasks for a goalie is to alertly follow all game situations and, through preventive actions, try to stop a goal situation from happening. The goalie should, therefore, through his or her play, control the entire penalty area and lead and direct the defense.

The goalie is a defender, but a talented goalie can also become an offensive player.

Whenever goalkeepers have the ball, they must think soccer in the same way as any other field player and capitalize on every situation to start an attack quickly. This should happen with exact passes, throws, or kicks to teammates in open areas of the field. To achieve this the goalie must have a good playing knowledge of the game.

Because the goalie's tasks differ so much from the other players, it is also recommended that he or she, as well as other athletes, get special practice at his or her job.

What Should the Goalie Practice?

Start with the selected goalie's special needs when you put together a coaching program. To be a good goalie, it is most important that he or she also learn the basics of the game. All play practices for seven- to nine-year-olds should be of help in teaching the basics. In addition, the goalie should practice in as many game situations as possible.

Let the goalie play in the goal almost all of the time the other players are drilled in plays. Don't forget that the goalie needs special coaching with the drills explained in this chapter at all practice sessions.

Suggestions for the Goalie

General

- Do not get sloppy with warm-ups. A good warm-up is the best insurance against injuries.
- Keep contact with the field players. Direct them and give them information so that there is always support and coverage at the opposing team's free kicks and corner kicks. Make sure that positions in these instances are known by you and by the field players.
- Direct players at practice. Your teammates should recognize your voice and understand you at all times.

- Follow the play at all times, stay alert.
- Make your moves appear as straightforward and clear as possible.
- Take full responsibility for your actions. Don't trust other players to save the situation for you.
- Practice as often as possible. Set your sights on being a good goalie and concentrate on individual coaching and practice.
- Practice as often as possible in goal so that you can control your position between the posts at all times.

Shots on Goal

- Control your position in relationship to the posts.
- Get good balance through good footwork.
- Always try to dive on the sides of your body. This will relieve the arms to catch the ball.
- Try to catch all balls. Punch or tip the ball only in desperate situations.
- Meet the shooter to cut down the angle of the shot (Figure 15.4).

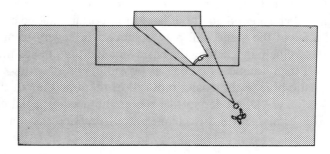

Figure 15.4 Goalie should cut down angle of shot.

Set Plays and Corner Kicks

- Your positioning is very important on corner kicks and set plays (free kicks). You must be able to break up an in-swinger at the near post and be prepared to go out and catch a long high ball (Figure 15.5).
- Learn to follow the ball pattern, there could be many players in your way.
- Always approach the ball. Don't stand and wait until it comes to you.
- When you attack the ball, you should have some power in your momentum so that you cannot be so easily pushed aside by others.

- Try to reach the ball as far out as possible.
- Talk to your teammates and let them know your moves. Yell "goalie" so that they know you are coming.

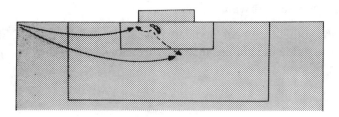

Figure 15.5 Goalie position for corner kicks.

Restart

- The tempo of the game is, for the most part, related to how fast you can restart the play.
- Whenever you catch a ball, restart the play toward the other side of the field. There are usually fewer players on that side.
- Roll and throw the ball as your first choice.
- Always take the goal kicks. It is unnecessary to give the opposing team a numerical advantage in these situations.
- Play the ball out to the sidelines. This is the best start-up possibility, and you can more easily reach your teammates.

Ongoing Play

- Don't stand between the posts when the ball is on the field. Utilize the entire penalty area.
- Direct your teammates.

Rushes

- If you believe that you can reach the ball before an opposing player, make a full effort, rush out, and get it.
- If you arrive at the same time, kick the ball away.
- If the opposing player has the ball under control, sneak out, cut off the angle, and observe the moves. Force the player to do what you

want him or her to do through a feint to one side. Be open on the side you want the player to play.

- Don't dive too early.
- Don't hesitate. Always be sure of yourself.
- Work yourself forward.

It is important that the coach dedicate proper time to the goalies. It is also important to guide the goalies through directions so that they can practice with each other.

| Exercise 1 | Goalie practice for ten- to fourteen-year-olds |

The Scoop: Ground Balls

Equipment:
1 ball, 8 cones
Area Size:
10 × 10 meters,
2 goals at
7 meters

B   A

Figure 15.6   The scoop: ground balls.

Organization
Goalie A rolls the ball straight to B, who scoops up the ball. B rolls the ball back to A, who picks it up in the scoop.

Instructions
The goalies assume the "basic position": stand with their feet apart, approximately the width of their shoulders, feet pointing straight forward. The knees should be a little flexed and the upper body bent slightly forward. The weight should be put on the balls of the feet.

From this position, the goalie takes a little wider stance when the ball is coming. Dropping the upper body and the lower arms with the outside of the hands touching the ground, the goalie scoops up the ball to the stomach (Figure 15.7).

Figure 15.7 The scoop: a close-up view.

Note. The goalie should not put a knee down on the ground when picking up the ball. He or she is then locked into that position and will have problems adjusting if the ball makes a diverting move.

Variations

- Roll the ball slowly at first, then increase the speed.
- Kick ground balls a meter to each side of the goalie.

Note. The goalie should move sideways with feet pointed forward. He or she cannot run sideways for the ball. The goalie should always try to get the body behind the ball when catching it.

Exercise 2   Goalie practice for ten- to fourteen-year-olds

The Scoop: Balls at Waist Height

Equipment:
1 ball, 8 cones
Area Size:
10 × 10 meters,
2 goals at 7 meters

B

A

Figure 15.8   The scoop: balls at waist height.

Organization
Goalie B throws the ball at waist height to A, who catches the ball and throws it back to B. The players catch the ball in the scoop.

Instructions
The goalie should stand in the basic position (See Exercise 1) and meet the ball with arms and hands, keeping the elbows together and the palms upward, meeting the ball, letting it in, and leaning slightly forward to absorb some shock with the body. The goalie should grab the ball with a sure grip while still keeping the elbows together so that the ball does not slip through.

Variations
- Throw underarm (softball pitch).
- Throw loose tosses over the head.
- Kick half volleys.
- Direct the ball a few meters to the side of the goalie.

Exercise 3   Goalie practice for ten- to fourteen-year-olds

The Scoop: Balls at Chest Height

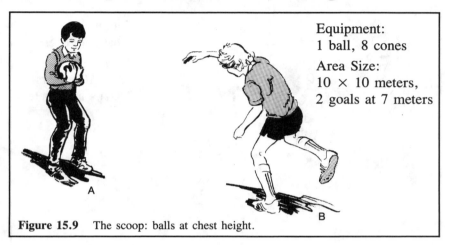

Equipment:
1 ball, 8 cones

Area Size:
10 × 10 meters,
2 goals at 7 meters

Figure 15.9   The scoop: balls at chest height.

Organization
Goalie B throws the ball at chest height to A, who gathers the ball into the scoop and throws it back to B. Continue with this practice.

Instructions
The goalie should stand in the basic position (see Exercise 1) and meet the ball with somewhat bent arms and open hands. Catch the ball with spread fingers and thumbs touching behind the ball. At the same time, give a little with the arms following the ball and softening the shock. Pull or gather the ball in. If this is done without sound, the technique is correct. After a catch, the ball is pulled into the scoop for safety.

Exercise 4	Goalie practice for ten- to fourteen-year-olds

Ball in the Scoop: Tackle

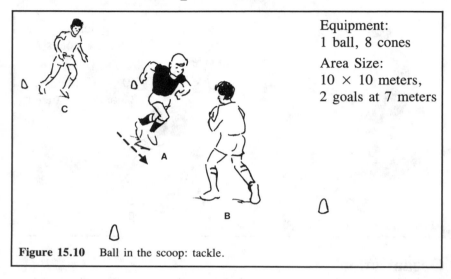

Equipment:
1 ball, 8 cones

Area Size:
10 × 10 meters,
2 goals at 7 meters

Figure 15.10   Ball in the scoop: tackle.

Organization

A throws or rolls the ball to B, who catches it in the scoop. A follows and tackles. B moves forward a few steps, and throws or rolls the ball to C, who catches it in the scoop. B follows through with a tackle.

Instructions

The goalies must grab the ball hard in the scoop. They cannot stand with feet too close together or they will easily lose balance at contact with the tackler.

<table>
<tr><td>Exercise 5</td><td>Goalie practice for ten- to fourteen-year-olds</td></tr>
</table>

The Scoop: High Balls

Equipment:
1 ball, 8 cones

Area Size:
10 × 10 meters,
2 goals at 7 meters

Figure 15.11   The scoop: high balls.

Organization
Goalie A throws a high ball to B, who catches the ball and throws back to A, who catches it again.

Instructions
The grip is the same for balls at chest height. To get power the goalie should catch the ball at the highest position possible, preferably somewhere in front of the vertical line created by the upright body. After the ball is caught it is pulled quickly down toward the body.

Variations
- Throw balls that the goalie can catch standing up.
- Throw balls that the goalie must jump for and catch at the highest point. Vary the jumps—both feet together and off one foot.
- Throw balls so that the goalie must meet and jump.
- Throw balls so that the goalie must back up and jump for them.
- Throw balls one meter to each side of the goalie.
- Throw balls that the goalie can catch sitting down.
- Throw balls that the goalie can catch in a prone position.

| Exercise 6 | Goalie practice for ten- to fourteen-year-olds |

Punch the Ball

Equipment:
1 ball, 6 cones

Area Size:
15 × 10 meters,
1 goal at 7 meters

A   B   C

Figure 15.12   Punch the ball.

Organization

A throws the ball in an arc toward the goal. B tries to reach it with the head. C is defending the goal and should punch the ball back to A. After ten throws the players change tasks: A is goalie, C tries to head, and B throws the ball.

Instructions

For precision the goalie should use both hands to punch the ball. He or she can reach further with only one hand but can expect poorer precision from the punch.

The goalie should use only one hand when it is hard to reach the ball. The fist should be very tight.

If the ball comes in an arc toward the goal and the situation is tight, the goalie can flip the ball over the crossbar with one palm.

Exercise 7   Goalie practice for ten- to fourteen-year-olds

Setup Head on Goal

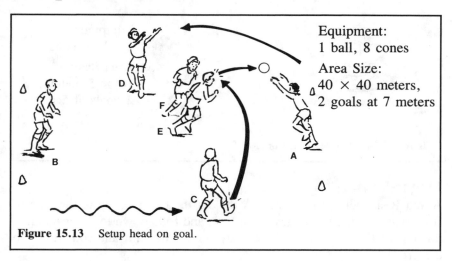

Equipment:
1 ball, 8 cones

Area Size:
40 × 40 meters,
2 goals at 7 meters

Figure 15.13   Setup head on goal.

Organization
C drives the ball toward the touchline and lays up a ball that E and F try to score. A takes the ball and throws it to D who drives the ball toward the other goal and lays up a pass that E and F try to score. B throws the ball to C and the exercise continues.

After six lay-ups, C and D change tasks with E and F. After awhile the exercise should be changed to the other direction so that the lay-ups come from the other side.

Instructions
The goalie should avoid starting a new attack on the side from which the ball comes. The opposing team usually has more players on that side.

| Exercise 8 | Goalie practice for ten- to fourteen-year-olds |

Fall Technique One

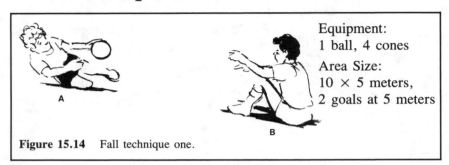

Equipment:
1 ball, 4 cones
Area Size:
10 × 5 meters,
2 goals at 5 meters

Figure 15.14   Fall technique one.

Organization
A and B sit facing each other. A throws the ball slightly to the side of B. B stretches the body, grabs the ball, and rolls down to the ground. B throws the ball. A stretches the body, grabs the ball, and rolls down to the ground.

Instructions
When goalies start learning fall techniques in this fashion, they don't have to worry about getting hurt. The fall is low. A goalie must also remember to pull the ball into the scoop as soon as it is caught and be sure to touch the ground only with the soft part of the body, with no knees or elbows on the ground.

Variations
- Throw the ball close to the body; the goalie must roll down and grab the ball.
- Throw the ball further from the body; the goalie must stretch out the body and finish as before.
- Throw ball far from the body so that the goalie must push for a second, losing contact with the ground before the ball is caught.
- Two goalies roll the ball to each other with hands and feet. They dive and catch each other's tosses.

Exercise 9   Goalie practice for ten- to fourteen-year-olds

Fall Technique Two

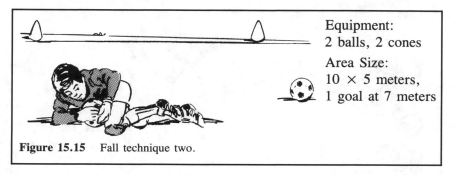

Equipment:
2 balls, 2 cones

Area Size:
10 × 5 meters,
1 goal at 7 meters

Figure 15.15   Fall technique two.

Organization

Two balls are placed one meter in front of each goal post. The goalie stands in the middle of the goal, moves sideways to a suitable position from one ball, falls down, grabs the ball, puts it down on its original place, and moves sideways to the next ball; and the exercise repeats.

Instructions

The goalie should start out by getting close to the ball and rolling down to grab it. Make sure the technique is correct from the beginning. The goalie should bend the knee closest to the ball, transfer weight to that leg, grab the ball, pull it into the scoop, lock the elbows, pull up both knees as close to the elbows as possible, and turn one side to the ground.

Exercise 10   Goalie practice for ten- to fourteen-year-olds

Squatting: Catch Bouncing Ball

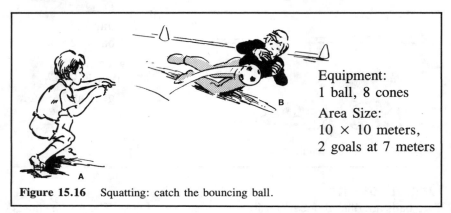

Equipment:
1 ball, 8 cones

Area Size:
10 × 10 meters,
2 goals at 7 meters

Figure 15.16   Squatting: catch the bouncing ball.

Organization
Goalie A and B squat facing each other. A bounces the ball several meters to the side of B. B dives, catches the ball, and bounces it back to A who dives to catch the ball.

Instructions
If your goalies get dirty knees and elbows, their fall techniques are wrong and you should give new instructions.

If a goalie is dirty on one side only (knees and elbows) you should coach him or her to dive correctly toward that side.

Exercise 11   Goalie practice for ten- to fourteen-year-olds

Goalie Match

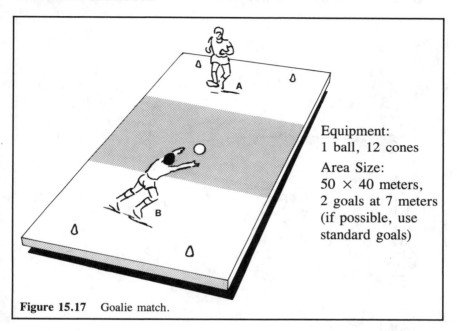

Equipment:
1 ball, 12 cones

Area Size:
50 × 40 meters,
2 goals at 7 meters
(if possible, use
standard goals)

Figure 15.17 Goalie match.

Organization
A plays the ball to B's penalty area. If A can get the ball to bounce before B touches the ball, A gets 1 point. If A scores a goal, 3 points are awarded.

Instructions
The goalies soon realize that it is not that dangerous to move out into the penalty area because they have time to move around during the flight of the ball.

The distance between the penalty areas can be shortened if needed. If there are no goal posts available, use cones.

Variations
- Goalie kicks a volley or half volley.
- Goalie throws the ball.
- Goalie kicks a stationary ball.

Exercise 12   Goalie practice for ten- to fourteen-year-olds

Score in the Triangle

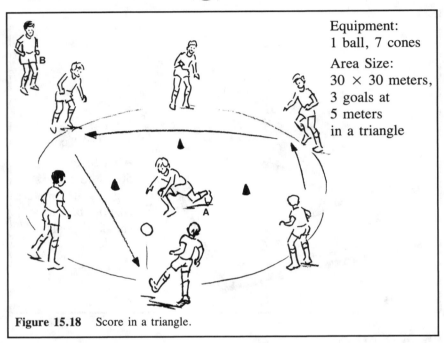

Equipment:
1 ball, 7 cones

Area Size:
30 × 30 meters,
3 goals at
5 meters
in a triangle

Figure 15.18   Score in a triangle.

Organization
Six players are in a ring and shoot the ball at one of the three goals. Goalie A tries to catch the shot. After a minute, goalie A changes with goalie B.

Instructions
Organizing the circle prevents the ball from going outside the area, and the goalie gets several shots in a short time. Don't allow too many blocks (direct return from the goalie without a catch). Rather, slow down the tempo.

If the goalie misses three times in a row, stop the exercise.

There are several reasons for constant misses:

- The goalie is tired; give him or her a fair chance.
- The instructions are not thorough enough.
- The level of difficulty is increased too soon.

Variations

- The players can pass only to each other three times before they shoot.
- The goalie can move between the goals.
- The goalie cannot go through the triangle.
- The players can pass the ball to each other unlimited times.

| Exercise 13 | Goalie practice for ten- to fourteen-year-olds |

Penalty Kick (Shoot-Out)

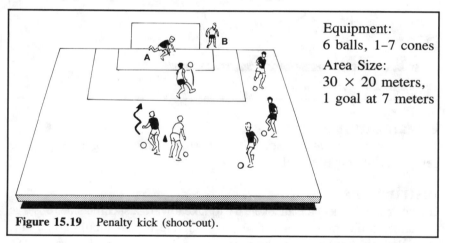

Equipment:
6 balls, 1–7 cones

Area Size:
30 × 20 meters,
1 goal at 7 meters

Figure 15.19   Penalty kick (shoot-out).

Organization

NASL games that were tied at the end of regulation time were decided as follows: A player starts with the ball thirty meters from the goal. He or she must score in five seconds, otherwise the attack is over.

The two goalies, A and B, take turns every other attack.

Instructions

The goalie should meet the attacker. He or she should also fake the shooter to move toward his or her stronger side. In addition, the goalie should wait and observe the attacker's moves and should not dive too early.

| Exercise 14 | Goalie practice for ten- to fourteen-year-olds |

Dribble and Shoot

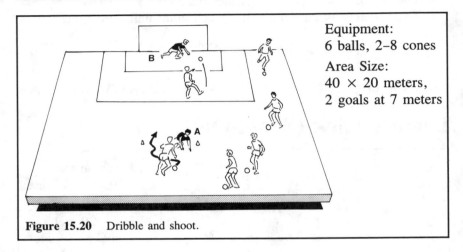

Equipment:
6 balls, 2–8 cones

Area Size:
40 × 20 meters,
2 goals at 7 meters

Figure 15.20 Dribble and shoot.

Organization
The attackers, one at a time, dribble past A in the first goal and try to get a shot off on B's goal.

Instructions
Goalie A should meet the attacker, try to fake toward a specific side, observe the selected moves, and not dive early. Goalie B also should come out, meet the attacker, and cut down the angle (as shown in Figure 15.4).

Show the goalie how to keep proper position between the posts at each new attack.

Exercise 15   Goalie practice for ten- to fourteen-year-olds

Four Against Two Plus One Goalie

Equipment:
4 balls, 4–6 cones

Area Size:
1 penalty area,
1 goal at 7 meters

Figure 15.21   Four against two plus one goalie.

Organization

B plays a ball to one of the attacking players. They play inside of the penalty area, trying to get into shooting position as quickly as possible, but they cannot move into the goalie area. The two defenders try to break up the pass or cover shots, after which they play back to A, who throws it to B. B will then play the ball in again.

After three minutes B becomes goalie and A takes over as set-up player.

Instructions

The goalie cannot play on the goal line, but must move out to cut down angles. There should be no attackers in the goalie area so that the goalie can work undisturbed.

Exercise 16	Goalie practice for ten- to fourteen-year-olds

Three Against Three With One Reserve Against One Goal

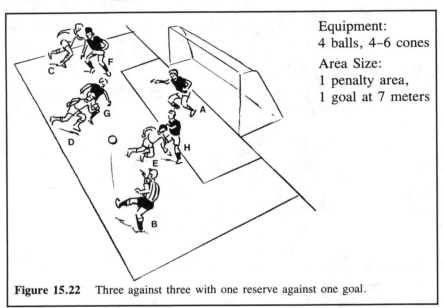

Equipment:
4 balls, 4–6 cones

Area Size:
1 penalty area,
1 goal at 7 meters

Figure 15.22   Three against three with one reserve against one goal.

Organization

C, D, and E play against F, G, and H inside the penalty area. B always belongs to the team that gets the ball when goalie A throws it backward overhead.

One team attacks until it has taken a shot on goal or until a defender gets the ball and plays it back to the goalie. If the ball goes outside the penalty area, the attacking team brings it back in and continues. After three minutes, B becomes goalie and A the set-up player.

Instructions

The goalie, as previously mentioned, should move out from the goal line and should have now learned to direct the defenders.

Metric Conversion Chart

Meters	Yards (approximate values)
120	130
110	120
100	110
90	100
75	80
64	70
45	50
16.5	18
11	12
9	10

Glossary

It is important that everyone engaged in soccer discussions, coaching, and other activities related to the sport speak the same language to express themselves. It is also important that the players understand and use the *proper soccer terminology*. This way they will better understand each other and the coach. The following is a list of the soccer terms used in this book and their explanations.

Attack. Whenever your team has ball, all players should be considered attackers.

Back Pass. The ball handler passes the ball backward to an unmarked teammate.

Center. (*See* Forwards.)

Challenge. The ball handler tries to get a one-on-one situation by driving the ball toward (rather than away from) an opposing player.

Combined Marking. This is a combination of zone and one-on-one. Whenever the opposing team starts an attack, the defenders mark players in their assigned zones. If the attacker changes, especially when close to the defending goal, the one-on-one takes over. If, however, the attacker changes zone in a quiet area or when the play is dead, the defenders should stay in their own zone and mark players in that zone.

Coverage. The further from the ball a player is, the looser the marking can be. The play area behind teammates should always be covered.

Create an Open Field. An attacking player moves, without the ball, toward an open space of the field. Through this move, the opposing player, for marking purposes, will leave areas open that the attacking team can then use. (Especially useful when wings stay very close to the sidelines.)

Cross Ball. Pass the ball from one wing to the other. This is a good way to "turn the play." (*See also* Turn the play.)

Defenders. Whenever the opposing team has the ball, your entire team takes a defensive posture and all become defenders.

Defending Area. When defending players place themselves between the ball and the defending goal, they create the defending area.

Directed Play. Coaching by which a play moment is a directed part in a play or small team play (e.g., wall pass gives one extra point in five against five). Could also mean restrictive coaching (e.g., two-touch practice). (*See also* Play moment.)

Dribbling. The ball handler tries to pass by an opposing player while keeping the ball under full control.

Drive the Ball. Run with the ball in an open area of the field.

Feinting. The ball handler will try to trick the opposing player into believing that he or she will do one thing, then he or she does another thing (e.g., fakes to the right but goes to the left).

Fixed or Set Plays. Corner kicks, throw-ins, free kicks, penalty kicks, kick offs, goal-kicks, and drop balls are all fixed, or set plays.

Fore-Checking. This is an offensive defense tactic; some players together check an entire fullback line.

Forwards (Wings and Centers). These are the front-line attacking positions; wings play close to the sidelines; centers play center field. Both positions are also called "forward." Wings are sometimes called "outside left or right forwards."

Fullback Line. Players closest to their own goal on eleven-person teams are often placed on a fullback line and called backs: outerbacks, innerbacks, and centerbacks.

Full Team Play. Terminology used in this book for seven-person teams on smaller fields for younger players and eleven-person teams for older players.

Halfbacks. (*See* Midfielders.)

Leaving. Leaving occurs whenever two players on the same team move toward one another, and the ball handler leaves the ball for the other player, who continues the play in the opposite direction.

Libero. The innerback who has no marking duties but is responsible for giving support and coverage, especially behind the marking innerback and the two outside backs, so he or she can take over whenever one of these is overplayed. Even in an attacking posture, the two innerbacks can have designated tasks (e.g., one of them can support the attack). (*See also* Marking innerbacks.)

Marking.   When marking an opponent, a defensive player stays on a line between the opposing player and his or her goal. Marking should be done closely, so that the player can break up a pass before the opposing player gets the ball.

Marking Innerbacks.   The two innerbacks often have a designated task in defensive plays. One of them, the marking innerback, marks an opposing forward, usually the center player (center halfback). (*See also* Libero.)

Midfielders.   Midfielders (also called halfbacks) play the central area of the field. There are right and left or outer and inner midfielders.

One-on-One Marking.   One player marks a specific player on the other team regardless of where the player is on the field.

Overlapping.   To overlap or come on the outside means that the ball handler gets help from a teammate who comes up from behind on the outside (either side). This creates a passing opportunity in play depth and creates width and opportunities to go around the defense.

Pass Feint.   Pass feint gives the ball handler an alternative to fake a pass or shoot in one direction, while he or she moves in another direction.

Passing Shadow.   Passing shadow is the area behind an opponent who is defending against (pressing) the ball handler. It is the area of the field to which the ball handler should not play the ball.

Play Coaching.   Coaching different plays (e.g., small team plays, play moment, etc.).

Play Depth.   Play depth means that the ball handler should have teammates both in front of (forward play depth) and behind (support in the attack) himself or herself.

Play Moment.   Coaching that involves isolating and practicing separately some part of the game (e.g., wall pass, pass from wings, etc.).

Play on a Marked Player.   The ball handler passes to a (mostly forward play depth) player who, with the back against the attacking goal, and even when marked or pressed, can receive the ball and play on or make a back pass to another teammate.

Play System.   This entails organizing the players so that the basics of attack and defense are accomplished, achieving fair task distribution, and utilizing the individual player's strength to its maximum potential.

Press. The attacking ball handler is slowed down by the closest defender and thereby has difficulty moving the ball forward. The purpose of the press is to slow down the pace and to give teammates a chance to get back into a defending position.

Second Wave. The distance between forward and the midfield cannot be too open. The midfield and backs must move up to give support, keeping the attack going. It's important at throw-ins and corner kicks to have a second wave of players so that the attack does not come to a stop if the defending team breaks up the play.

Setup Play. The players control the ball within their own side of the field (set up an attack), using a predesigned play.

Small Team Play. Games that are played with teams of fewer than seven and eleven players (e.g., five vs. five, four vs. two, etc.).

Speed. The speed a player has in the game is a combination of thinking quickly and moving quickly.

Support. In defending situations, one player is positioned behind, but not too close to, a teammate who is the pressing player. Whenever the pressing player is overplayed, the next defensive player takes over (gives support).

Tactic. Tactic means that the team play is adjusted to the situation governing the game.

Turn the Play. In attacking posture, players move the play from a bad area of the field to a better one. This happens mostly from one side to the other (i.e. left to right).

Wall Play. Wall play is built on a two-on-one situation. The ball handler passes the ball to a free player on one side, rushes by the defender, and receives the ball back from the wall (the other player). The important factor of this play is that the wall must pass the ball back quickly and well in front of the teammate.

Wings. (*See* Forwards.)

Zone Marking. This is done within designated areas of the field. Players are responsible for their zone and should mark players moving into that zone. Zone area varies depending on the opposing players' positions. The defensive players change assignments when the opposing player changes zone.